GAO

Report to the Ranking Minority Member, Committee on Commerce, House of Representatives

May 2000

PIPELINE SAFETY

The Office of Pipeline Safety Is Changing How It Oversees the Pipeline Industry

GAO/RCED-00-128

Contents

Abbreviations

OPS   Office of Pipeline Safety
DOT   Department of Transportation

GAO
Accountability * Integrity * Reliability

United States General Accounting Office
Washington, D.C. 20548

B-283653

May 15, 2000

The Honorable John D. Dingell
Ranking Minority Member
Committee on Commerce
House of Representatives

Dear Mr. Dingell:

Pipelines are inherently safer to the public than other modes of freight transportation for natural gas and hazardous liquids (such as oil products) because they are, for the most part, located underground. Nevertheless, the volatile nature of these products means that pipeline accidents can have serious consequences. For example, when a pipeline ruptured and spilled about 250,000 gallons of gasoline into a creek in Bellingham, Washington, in June 1999, three people were killed, eight were injured, several buildings were damaged, and the banks of the creek were destroyed along a 1.5-mile section.

The Office of Pipeline Safety, within the Department of Transportation, administers the national regulatory program to ensure the safe transportation of natural gas and hazardous liquids by pipeline. The Office has traditionally carried out its responsibility by issuing minimum standards and enforcing them uniformly across these pipelines. The Accountable Pipeline Safety and Partnership Act of 1996 directed the Office to establish a demonstration program to test a risk management approach to pipeline safety. This approach involves identifying and addressing specific risks faced by individual pipeline companies rather than applying uniform standards regardless of risks. The act allowed the Office to exempt companies in the program from the uniform standards but did not eliminate the standards.

Concerned about the recent accident in Bellingham, you asked us to review the Office's performance in regulating pipeline safety. Accordingly, we examined (1) the extent of major pipeline accidents from 1989 through 1998 (the most recent data available), (2) the Office's implementation of the 1996 act's risk management demonstration program, (3) the Office's inspection and enforcement efforts since the act's implementation, and (4) the Office's responsiveness to recommendations from the National Transportation Safety Board (the Safety Board) and to statutory requirements designed to improve pipeline safety. In addition, you asked us to provide information on the current status of the investigation of the accident in Bellingham. This latter information is provided in appendix I.

Results in Brief

From 1989 through 1998, pipeline accidents resulted in an average of about 22 fatalities per year. Fatalities from pipeline accidents are relatively low when compared with those from accidents involving other forms of freight transportation: On average, about 66 people die each year from barge accidents, about 590 from railroad accidents, and about 5,100 from truck accidents. While these statistics provide an indication of the relative safety of pipelines for transporting natural gas and hazardous liquids, the total number of major pipeline accidents (those resulting in a fatality, an injury, or property damage of $50,000 or more) increased by about 4 percent annually over this 10-year period. Most fatalities and injuries occurred as a result of accidents on pipelines that transport natural gas to homes and businesses (primarily intrastate pipelines), while most property damage occurred as a result of accidents on pipelines transporting hazardous liquids (primarily interstate pipelines). Furthermore, pipelines that transport hazardous liquids account for nearly eight times as many major accidents per mile of pipeline as do pipelines that transport natural gas to homes and businesses. The Office of Pipeline Safety's data on the causes of pipeline accidents are limited to a few categories, but these limited data indicate that damage from outside forces, such as excavation, is the primary cause of such accidents.

The Office has implemented a risk management demonstration program, as the 1996 act requires, and has approved six demonstration projects, which are ongoing. The Office issued guidance on performance measures for the overall program and for individual projects but has not established specific measures of the program's impact on safety, as the act requires. Even though the projects are not complete and their safety benefits have not been quantified, the Office is moving ahead with a risk-based approach to safety regulation based partially on preliminary qualitative results of the program. Specifically, the Office has proposed a rule that would require some companies that operate hazardous liquid pipelines that run through high-risk areas (populated areas, environmentally sensitive areas, and commercially navigable waterways) to implement a program to comprehensively examine pipelines in these areas to identify and address potential risks, including assessing the current condition of their pipelines. The proposed rule will supplement, not replace, the existing minimum standards. The Office also plans to take several actions that are necessary to implement the new approach, such as devising a method to review the companies' programs and hiring and training additional staff to conduct the reviews. Office officials estimate that pipeline companies will develop plans for assessing the condition of their pipelines by September 2001 and that the assessments will be complete by September 2007. While we agree that a risk management approach offers the potential to improve pipeline safety, several critical steps—such as issuing a final rule and hiring staff—must be completed before the Office can implement such an approach.

Since the act's implementation, the Office has modified its inspection and enforcement approach. With respect to inspections, it has moved toward inspecting entire pipelines rather than segments of pipelines. Since 1996, the Office has decreased its use of "unit" inspections—inspections of individual pipeline segments—and has begun inspecting companies' entire pipeline operating systems at one time to provide more comprehensive assessments of safety risks. As a result, the Office has reduced its reliance on states to inspect interstate pipelines because it is difficult to coordinate participation by individual states in systemwide inspections. However, state pipeline safety officials who currently inspect interstate pipelines for the Office are concerned that their diminishing role has resulted in fewer and less thorough inspections of pipelines. The Office has also revised its enforcement of compliance with regulations by reducing its use of fines and, instead, working with operators to identify and correct safety problems. From 1990 to 1998, the Office decreased the proportion of enforcement actions in which it proposed fines from about 49 percent to about 4 percent. Some state safety regulators agree with this strategy; others do not. We are recommending that the Secretary of Transportation direct the Office to work with states to determine how state inspectors could be used to more effectively oversee pipeline safety and evaluate the effectiveness of its strategy of reducing the use of fines.

The Office's responsiveness to the Safety Board's recommendations and statutory requirements has been mixed. The Office has historically had the lowest rate of implementation for these recommendations of any transportation agency and has not implemented 22 statutory requirements, 12 of which date from 1992 or earlier. It has not implemented some of the recommendations and requirements because it believes they would be too costly for the pipeline industry compared with the expected benefits. However, according to the Safety Board, some of the Office's analyses of costs and benefits are flawed because the Office did not consider all of the benefits. The Office has recently taken action on some issues covered by outstanding recommendations and requirements, such as identifying countermeasures for preventing damage to pipelines from excavation and requiring pipeline operators to inspect their pipelines for corrosion. Safety Board officials say they are encouraged by these recent efforts but note that some of the Office's actions are incomplete and may not fully address the Safety Board's recommendations.

Background

Pipelines transport the bulk of natural gas and hazardous liquids (such as oil products) in the United States.[1] Specifically, pipelines carry nearly all of the natural gas and about 65 percent of the crude oil and refined oil products. Three primary types of pipelines form a network of nearly 2.2 million miles.

- Natural gas transmission pipelines transport natural gas over long distances from sources to communities. These pipelines—about 325,000 miles—are primarily interstate.
- Natural gas distribution pipelines continue to transport natural gas from transmission pipelines to residential, commercial, and industrial customers. These pipelines—about 1.7 million miles—are primarily intrastate.
- Hazardous liquid pipelines transport crude oil to refineries and continue to transport the refined oil product, such as gasoline, to product terminals and airports. These pipelines—about 156,000 miles—are primarily interstate.

In addition, pipelines include several components that aid in the collection and transportation of products. (See fig. 1.) For example, gathering pipelines collect natural gas or crude oil from producing wells and carry the product to a natural gas transmission or hazardous liquid pipeline.[2] Compressor stations (for gas) and pumping stations (for liquids) keep the product flowing smoothly.

---

[1] Hazardous liquid pipelines carry products such as crude oil, diesel fuel, gasoline, jet fuel, anhydrous ammonia, and carbon dioxide.

[2] Some gathering lines and segments of gathering lines in rural areas are excluded from federal pipeline safety regulation. The Office is developing a definition of natural gas gathering lines that may result in the regulation of some rural gathering lines. The mileage statistics above include gathering lines that are subject to federal regulation.

Figure 1: Components of Natural Gas Transmission and Distribution Pipelines

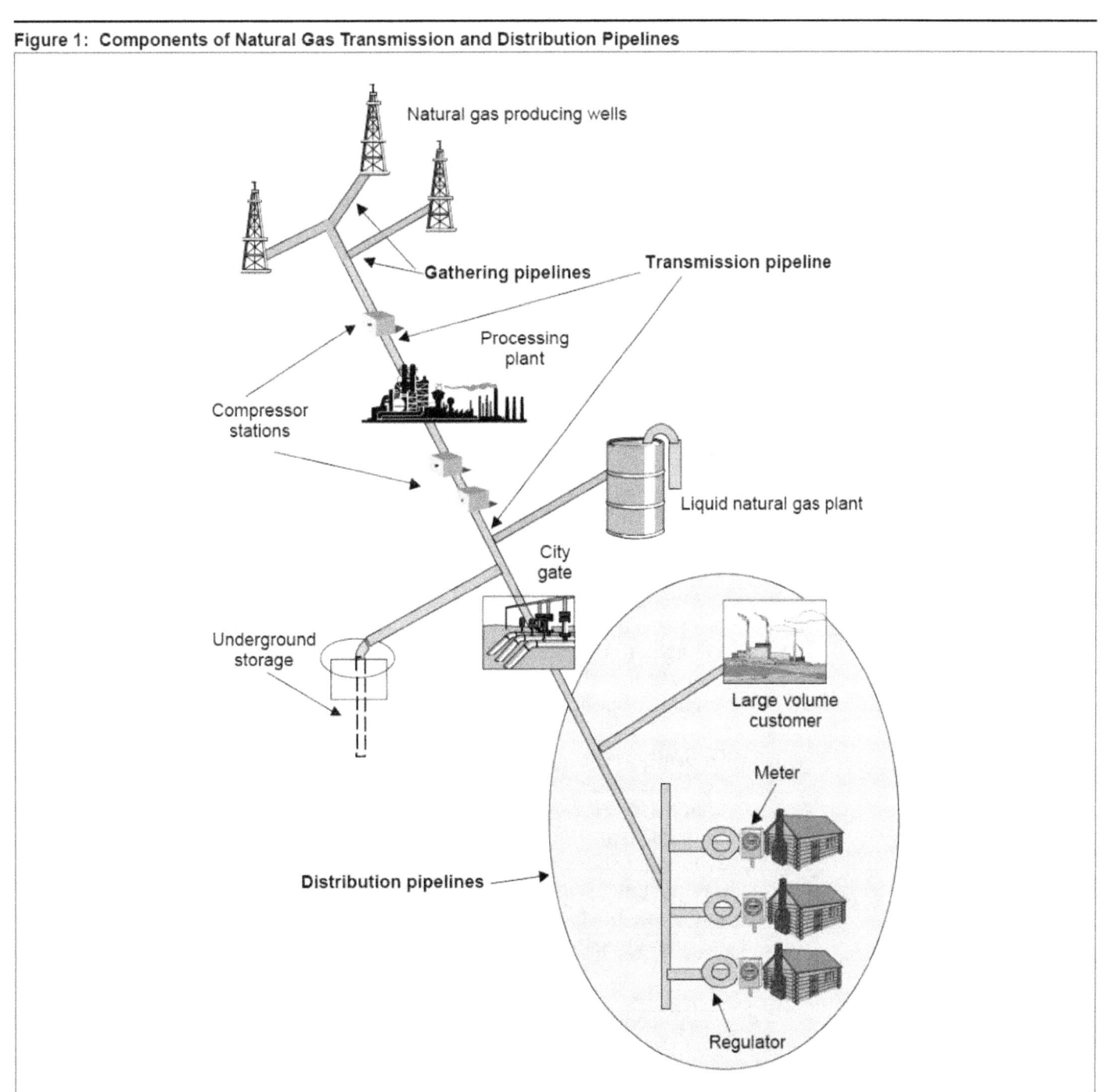

Source: Office of Pipeline Safety.

GAO/RCED-00-128 Oversight of Pipeline Safety

The extensive network of natural gas transmission and hazardous liquid pipelines appears in appendix II.[3]

Several federal and state agencies have roles in pipeline safety. The Office of Pipeline Safety (OPS) develops, issues, and enforces pipeline safety regulations for natural gas and hazardous liquid pipelines. These regulations contain minimum safety standards that the pipeline companies that transport these products must meet for the design, construction, inspection, testing, operation, and maintenance of pipelines. OPS' fiscal year 2000 budget is about $37 million, funded primarily from industry user fees. In fiscal year 1999, OPS employed 105 people, 51 of whom were pipeline inspectors.

In general, OPS retains full responsibility for inspecting and enforcing regulations on interstate pipelines but certifies states to perform these functions for intrastate pipelines. Certified states are allowed to impose safety requirements for intrastate pipelines that are stricter than the federal regulations. As of March 2000, 47 state agencies, the District of Columbia, and Puerto Rico were certified for intrastate natural gas pipeline inspections, and 12 state agencies were certified for intrastate hazardous liquid pipeline inspections.[4] Certified states are authorized to receive reimbursement of up to 50 percent of the costs of their pipeline safety programs from OPS. In fiscal year 1999, these states received about $13 million from OPS in state pipeline safety grants, or an average of about 44 percent of their estimated budgets. In fiscal year 1998, the states employed about 300 pipeline inspectors.

OPS also uses some states to help inspect interstate pipelines. These states, or "interstate agents," inspect segments of interstate pipelines within their boundaries. However, OPS handles any enforcement actions identified through inspections conducted by these interstate agents. As of March 2000, eight states were acting as interstate agents—five states for natural gas pipelines, one state for hazardous liquid pipelines, and two states for both types of pipelines. These states do not receive additional federal funds for inspecting interstate pipelines.

---

[3]No map is available for the natural gas distribution pipeline network, which is too extensive to map because it is located in populated areas.

[4]In addition, four state agencies—Delaware for natural gas and Kentucky, New Mexico, and South Carolina for hazardous liquid—have agreements with OPS to inspect intrastate pipelines, but OPS handles any enforcement actions.

Other federal agencies, such as the Minerals Management Service within the Department of the Interior and the Environmental Protection Agency, also have some regulatory authority related to pipeline safety. The Minerals Management Service has jurisdiction over producer-operated oil pipelines on the Outer Continental Shelf. The Environmental Protection Agency regulates tanks used to store hazardous liquids or transfer them to or from other modes of transportation. In contrast, OPS regulates storage tanks used to store hazardous liquids for continued transportation by pipeline at a later date or to relieve surges in the pipeline system. A single storage tank or a facility with multiple tanks may have uses that fall under the authority of both the Environmental Protection Agency and OPS. As of April 2000, the agencies were working to clarify the circumstances under which each agency has authority.

The National Transportation Safety Board investigates transportation accidents, including significant pipeline accidents (such as those involving fatalities). On the basis of these investigations, the Safety Board issues recommendations to OPS and other federal agencies aimed at preventing future accidents. Finally, several federal statutes enacted since 1988 contain requirements designed to improve pipeline safety and enhance OPS' ability to oversee the pipeline industry. Many of these requirements address the same issues as the Safety Board's recommendations.

Pipelines Are Relatively Safe, but the Number of Major Accidents Increased From 1989 Through 1998

Pipelines have an inherent safety advantage over other modes of freight transportation because they are primarily located underground, away from public contact. From 1989 through 1998, pipeline accidents resulted in an average of about 22 fatalities per year, compared with about 66 from barge accidents, about 590 from railroad accidents, and about 5,100 from large truck accidents.[5] A 1999 study comparing modes of oil transportation from 1992 through 1997—pipeline, rail, tank ship, barge, and truck—found that the likelihood of fatality, injury, or fire and/or explosion is generally lowest for pipelines.[6] The rate of fatalities, injuries, and fires/explosions per ton-mile of oil transported for all other modes is typically at least twice—and in

---

[5]In its regulations, OPS refers to the release of natural gas from a pipeline as an "incident" and a spill from a hazardous liquid pipeline as an "accident." For simplicity, this report will refer to both as "accidents."

[6]Cheryl J. Trench, *The U.S. Oil Pipeline Industry's Safety Performance*, Allegro Energy Group report prepared for the Association of Oil Pipelines and the American Petroleum Institute (May 1999) (Rev.).

some cases more than 10 times—as great as the rate for pipelines. (See table 1.)

Table 1: Relative Occurrence of Transportation Accidents Per Ton-Mile of Oil Transported, 1992-97

Event	Pipeline[a]	Rail	Tank ship	Barge	Truck
Fatality	1.0	2.7	4.0	10.2	87.3
Injury	1.0	2.6	0.7	0.9	2.3
Fire/explosion	1.0	8.6	1.2	4.0	34.7

[a]The rates of occurrence are based on a value of 1.0 for pipeline. Values of less than 1.0 indicate a better safety record.

Source: Association of Oil Pipelines.

While pipelines are relatively safe compared with other transportation modes, the number of major pipeline accidents increased overall from 1989 through 1998.[7] In total, there were 2,241 major accidents (those causing a fatality, an injury, or more than $50,000 in property damage) during this period. Although the number of major accidents varied from year to year, these accidents increased by approximately 4 percent annually.[8] (See fig. 2.) According to OPS officials, the increase in major accidents over this period can be attributed to a 10-percent overall increase in pipeline mileage, growth in the volume of products transported by pipelines (due to an increase in the nation's energy consumption), and population growth near pipelines.

---

[7]All natural gas and hazardous liquid pipeline operators are required to report accidents that result in a fatality, an injury, or $50,000 or more in property damage (which this report defines as "major"). In addition, natural gas pipeline operators are required to report events that result in an emergency shutdown of a liquefied natural gas facility and may report any accident they consider "significant," even if it does not meet any reporting threshold. Furthermore, hazardous liquid operators are required to report any accident that results in an explosion or a fire, the release of 50 or more barrels of hazardous liquid or carbon dioxide, or the escape into the atmosphere of more than 5 barrels per day of highly volatile liquids. There were 1,801 accidents from 1989 through 1998 that did not meet the definition of a major accident.

[8]The total number of accidents, major and nonmajor, reported to OPS decreased by about 1.5 percent annually over this period.

Figure 2: Number of Pipeline Accidents Resulting In Fatalities, Injuries, and/or $50,000 or More In Property Damage, 1989-98

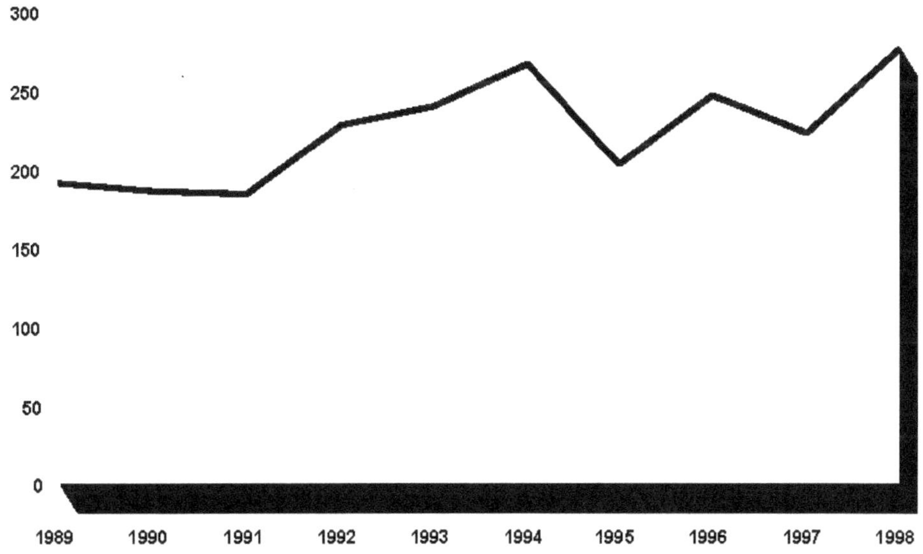

Source: GAO's analysis of OPS' data.

From 1989 through 1998, 226 people died and 1,030 people were injured in major pipeline accidents.[9] (See fig. 3.) Accidents on natural gas distribution pipelines (which are primarily intrastate) accounted for 173—or 77 percent—of the fatalities and 743—or 72 percent—of the injuries from 1989 through 1998. Because these pipelines are primarily located in populous areas, it is not surprising that accidents on them affect humans more than accidents on other types of pipelines. In addition, major pipeline accidents caused about $700 million in property damage. From 1989 through 1998, hazardous liquid pipelines (which are primarily interstate) accounted for about $350 million, or 50 percent, of this property damage

---

[9]This figure does not include the injuries that occurred during one series of accidents caused by severe flooding near Houston, Texas, in Oct. 1994. We excluded these injuries because OPS' and the Safety Board's data disagree on the number of people injured. OPS' data indicate 1,851 injuries, while the Safety Board reported that a total of 547 persons were treated, primarily for smoke and vapor inhalation. We also excluded this accident from our analysis because we could not determine to what extent the injuries were the result of explosions of petroleum and petroleum products released from the ruptured pipelines or of the controlled burn of these products by the spill response team.

because the liquids do not dissipate into the atmosphere, as does natural gas.

Figure 3: Number of Fatalities and Injuries and Amount of Property Damage From Pipeline Accidents, 1989-98

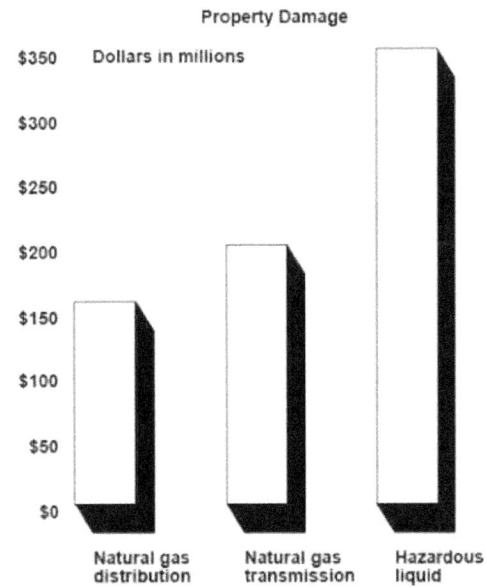

Source: GAO's analysis of OPS' data.

Representatives from environmental groups believe that property damage from pipeline accidents is understated because not all damage to the environment may be reported to OPS by pipeline operators. For example, over 1.5 million barrels of hazardous liquids—primarily crude oil and gasoline—were spilled from pipelines as a result of all pipeline accidents reported to OPS. However, the total amount spilled from pipelines and, thus, the environmental damage, is actually greater because OPS does not require pipeline operators to report spills of less than 50 barrels. Although there is no complete source of information on these smaller spills, the Environmental Protection Agency maintains data on oil pipeline spills in areas where such spills could cause pollution to navigable waters. These data show that more than 16,000 spills of less than 50 barrels occurred from 1989 through 1998.

Of the major pipeline accidents occurring from 1989 through 1998, most—about 43 percent—occurred on natural gas distribution pipelines. These pipelines also account for the majority of pipeline mileage. However, hazardous liquid pipelines, which account for the smallest portion of total pipeline mileage, have nearly eight times as many major accidents per mile of pipeline as do natural gas distribution pipelines. (See fig. 4.)

Figure 4: Number of Major Pipeline Accidents, Miles, and Major Accidents per 10,000 Miles of Pipeline, 1989-98

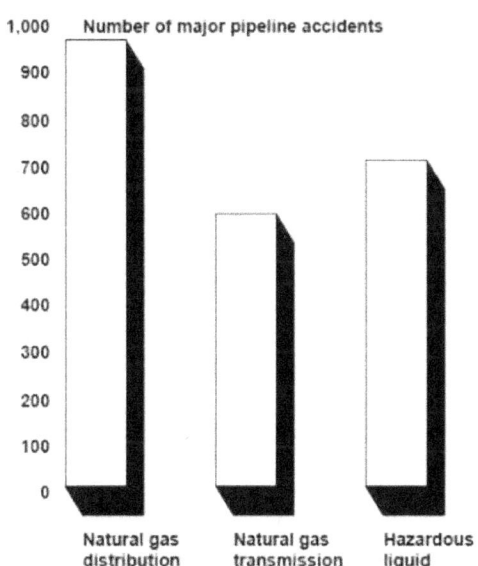

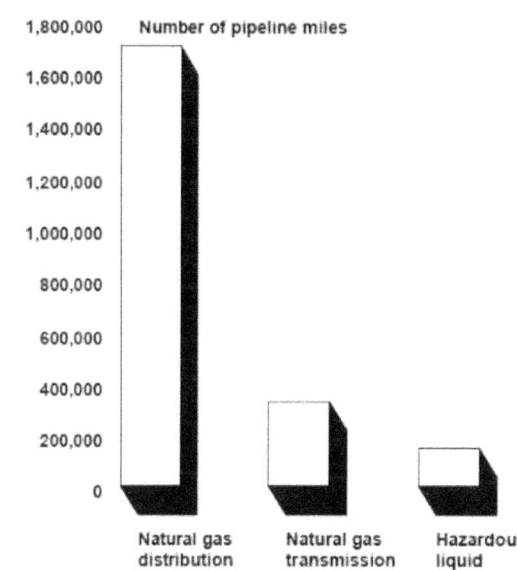

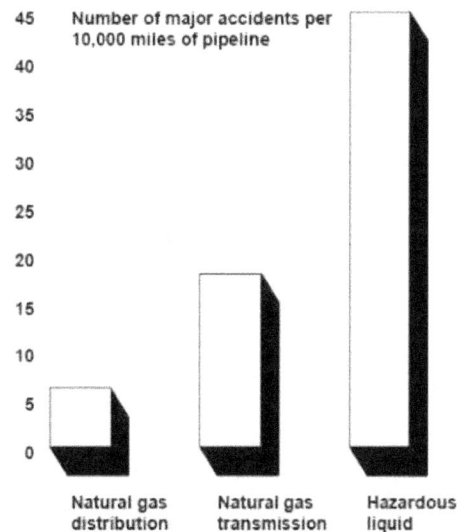

Source: GAO's analysis of OPS' data.

OPS does not collect comprehensive information on the causes of pipeline accidents. However, OPS' available data indicate that the primary cause of pipeline accidents from 1989 through 1998 was damage from external forces, such as an outside party digging near a pipeline or a natural force like an earthquake or a landslide. These data are limited because OPS uses only five categories of causes for accidents on natural gas distribution pipelines, four categories for those on natural gas transmission pipelines, and seven categories for those on hazardous liquid pipelines. As a result, a large proportion of accidents are attributed to "other causes" that range from failed gaskets or seals to faulty valves. According to these data, from 1989 through 1998, the three most prevalent causes of pipeline accidents were damage from outside forces (45 percent), "other" (25 percent), and corrosion of the pipe (15 percent).

Although Benefits of Demonstration Program Have Not Been Quantified, OPS Is Moving Ahead With a New Regulatory Approach

As a result of the Accountable Pipeline Safety and Partnership Act of 1996, OPS has implemented a risk management demonstration program to investigate whether formalized risk management programs for individual pipeline companies can provide an alternative to the current regulatory approach and achieve a superior level of safety and environmental protection.[10] However, OPS has not established performance measures for the program's impact on safety, as required by the act. OPS maintains that the ongoing program has already produced some qualitative improvements, such as directing resources to the areas posing the greatest safety risks. Partially as a result of its experience with the demonstration program, OPS has proposed a rule that would require some companies that operate hazardous liquid pipelines that run through populated areas, environmentally sensitive areas, or commercially navigable waterways to implement a program to comprehensively examine pipelines in these areas to identify and address potential risks.

---

[10]The act also required, among other things, that OPS conduct risk assessments when prescribing new regulations. In addition to identifying the costs and benefits of the new regulation, OPS must identify the regulatory and nonregulatory options considered, explain its reasons for choosing the selected option instead of the others, and identify the information on which the risk assessment and selected option are based. The status of OPS' actions on these additional requirements is included in app. IV.

Risk Management Demonstration Program Was Designed to Show Benefits of Going Beyond Minimum Regulatory Standards

The 1996 act, together with a presidential memorandum to the Secretary of Transportation, requires OPS to evaluate, through a demonstration program, whether a risk management approach to pipeline safety can achieve a level of safety and environmental protection that is greater than the level achievable through compliance with the current pipeline safety regulations.[11] The current regulations establish minimum safety requirements for all pipeline companies, such as a requirement for a protective coating on all pipelines to mitigate corrosion. A risk management approach goes beyond the minimum requirements by identifying and focusing resources on risks to individual pipelines that may not be fully addressed in the regulations. For example, identifying emergency response capability as a risk and subsequently developing an electronic system that would notify emergency officials of a pipeline leak or rupture would exceed current regulations.

The act further required OPS to develop performance measures for the program to evaluate its safety and environmental benefits. The act also authorized OPS to exempt companies participating in these projects from all or a portion of the existing regulations.[12] Finally, the act required OPS to report by March 31, 2000, on the results of the demonstration program, including its safety and environmental benefits.

To address the requirement for demonstrating an improved level of safety and environmental benefits, OPS issued guidance that identified superior safety, environmental protection, and service reliability as one of three primary objectives for the program. The guidance also identified increased efficiency of pipeline operations and improved communication among industry, government, and other stakeholders as two additional primary objectives. To measure progress toward these objectives, the guidance

---

[11]The 1996 act contained no limitation on the number of demonstration projects and required that risk management plans be designed to achieve a level of safety equivalent to or greater than the level that would otherwise be achieved. However, when signing the 1996 act, the President directed the Secretary of Transportation to limit the number of projects to 10 and to ensure that the projects demonstrate superior, not just equal, safety and environmental benefits.

[12]One company that operates a natural gas pipeline has received an exemption from the current regulations. If the population density increases near a pipeline, the current regulations require the pipeline company to install a thicker-walled pipe or reduce the operating pressure. In exchange for the exemption from this requirement, OPS is requiring the company to take additional precautions, such as conducting internal inspections of the pipelines in these areas, while maintaining the existing pipe at the original pressure.

describes potential programwide measures, such as accident data, risk awareness, and customer service. The guidance also recognizes the need for project-specific measures intended to document starting conditions, changes during the program, and expected outcomes for each project. According to the guidance, the project-specific measures were to be developed by the pipeline operators before the projects were approved by OPS.

As of January 2000, OPS had approved six projects for the program. The projects vary in scope, ranging from examining the risks associated with excavation work on a single pipeline at one company, to a comprehensive risk management plan designed to assess all risks associated with the operation of two multistate pipeline systems owned by another company. (App. III provides more details on the individual projects and the program's overall costs.)

OPS Has Not Measured Benefits of Risk Management Demonstration Program

OPS has not complied with the act's requirements or its own guidance on developing performance measures for the risk management demonstration program. Specifically, OPS has not developed programwide measures and has approved five of the six demonstration projects without project-specific measures in place, even though OPS' guidance required pipeline operators to develop such measures before the agency would approve a project. OPS officials and representatives of participating companies told us that they have been unable to develop performance measures because the impact on safety cannot easily be isolated from the effects of other safety activities outside the program, especially given the relatively short duration of the program. For example, an increase in the number of defects found over a period of years may indicate a growing risk of pipeline failure, or it may reflect the results of targeting inspections to identify weaknesses or of introducing new technologies to detect defects. In addition, OPS officials told us that the measures have been difficult to develop because the participating companies have unique pipeline systems and the demonstration projects involve different aspects of the systems. Moreover, according to the officials, many companies are not collecting the types of data necessary to support an evaluation of the program's overall impact on safety.

Only one program participant, Philips Pipe Line, has developed performance measures and generated data for its project. According to OPS officials, this project is limited in scope and has thus far generated little data. The other participants are trying to develop performance measures for their projects.

While OPS has not developed any programwide or project-specific measures to evaluate the program's performance, OPS officials told us that the program has yielded many qualitative benefits related to its three objectives. For example, each company is performing safety activities that exceed the requirements in the current regulations, such as conducting periodic internal inspections of pipelines and installing additional valves to prevent hazardous liquids from flowing into rivers. Officials with one company said that the company has allocated its resources more effectively by using a risk-based computer model to develop funding priorities for its valve modification and replacement efforts. To improve communication and information flow, two companies have conducted "hands-on" workshops for OPS, and another company is developing a computerized method of exchanging information with OPS.

Although the act required OPS to issue a report on the results of the demonstration program in March 2000, OPS plans to issue a report in spring 2000 on the progress of the program. OPS officials do not know when the program will be complete. According to OPS officials, the projects took longer to implement than planned because, among other things, (1) the participating companies did not already have vigorous, formalized risk management programs in place; (2) OPS took longer than expected to review and approve individual projects; and (3) several of the applicant companies underwent corporate mergers that created uncertainties about whether the companies would continue to participate in the program.

OPS Is Moving to Implement Risk Management Into Its Regulatory Framework

Even though the demonstration program is still ongoing and its safety and environmental benefits have not yet been quantified, OPS has proposed a rule that draws, in part, on the agency's experiences with the demonstration program to incorporate the use of a risk management approach in pipeline safety regulations.[13] The proposed rule would affect hazardous liquid pipeline companies (companies that operate systems of 500 miles or more) that have pipelines in "high-consequence areas." The rule defines these areas as populated areas, environmentally sensitive areas, or commercially navigable waterways.[14] OPS estimates that the rule would apply to 66 pipeline companies that operate about 87 percent of the nation's hazardous liquid pipeline mileage. All pipeline operators would still be required to follow the current minimum regulations.

Companies affected by this rule would be required to develop an "integrity management program" to comprehensively examine pipelines in high-consequence areas to identify and address potential risks. Such a program would include, among other things, (1) a plan for assessing the condition of pipelines in these areas, (2) periodic reassessments of the pipelines, (3) criteria for repairing deficiencies discovered through the assessments, and (4) measures of the program's effectiveness. Methods to assess the condition of the pipelines include internal inspections using "smart pigs" (devices that can travel through the pipelines to detect flaws) and hydrostatic testing (draining the pipeline, filling it with water, and increasing the pressure within the pipeline to identify weak points).

OPS intends to review companies' integrity management programs, including the risks identified by the companies and their strategies for addressing the risks. Although OPS officials have not determined exactly how these reviews will be integrated into the agency's periodic inspections of pipeline companies, they told us the reviews would require additional personnel. OPS officials could not estimate how many additional staff would eventually be needed. The agency has requested four additional staff

---

[13]The proposed rule also draws on the agency's experiences in inspecting pipeline companies' entire operating systems (described in the next section), investigating accidents, and conducting system integrity initiatives.

[14]According to OPS officials, the initial rule would affect operators of large hazardous liquid pipeline systems because OPS has gained familiarity with their operations through the risk management demonstration program. Subsequent rules would affect operators of small hazardous liquid pipelines and natural gas transmission pipelines in high-consequence areas.

for fiscal year 2001, and OPS officials expect to request more in future years. In addition, agency officials told us that OPS is considering hiring contractors to assist with these reviews.

Several actions must occur before OPS can fully implement this new approach to regulating pipeline safety. OPS issued a proposed rule on April 24, 2000, and must incorporate comments from the industry and the public in a final rule. OPS must also complete another rule on the definition of areas that are unusually sensitive to environmental damage before it can identify high-consequence areas.[15] In addition, OPS must develop guidelines for reviewing companies' integrity management programs and hire and train the additional staff needed to conduct the reviews. Meanwhile, the companies that have pipelines in high-consequence areas must develop their programs and assess the current condition of their pipelines. OPS estimates that pipeline companies will develop plans for assessing the condition of their pipelines by September 2001 and that the assessments will be complete by September 2007. (See table 2.)

Table 2: Milestones for Implementing a Risk Management Approach for Regulating Large Hazardous Liquid Pipelines

Date	Action
April 2000	OPS issued a proposed rule requiring enhanced protection of high-consequence areas
October 2000	OPS issues the final rule
Beginning October 2000	OPS hires and trains additional staff to review companies' integrity management programs
December 2000	OPS completes the final rule on the definition of areas unusually sensitive to environmental damage and makes mapping information available to pipeline companies on the Internet
September 2001	Pipeline companies complete plans for assessing the condition of pipelines
September 2004	Individual companies' assessments are 50 percent complete
September 2007	Assessments are 100 percent complete

Source: GAO's analysis of OPS' data.

---

[15]OPS issued a proposed rule on the definition of areas unusually sensitive to environmental damage on Dec. 30, 1999. Comments on the proposed rule are due by June 27, 2000.

While we agree that a risk management approach offers the potential to improve pipeline safety, we believe that OPS' proposed rule to broadly implement it is not supported by quantifiable evidence (intended to be obtained through the demonstration program) that such an approach has led—or could lead—to a higher level of safety and environmental protection. In addition, OPS plans to require performance measures for pipeline companies' integrity management programs, even though OPS and pipeline operators were not able to develop such measures for the risk management demonstration program. Nevertheless, the rulemaking process could give the safety community, the regulated industry, and affected states and communities the opportunity to shape the final rule so as to establish evidence of the approach's impact on safety and provide for reporting on outcomes and periodic assessments of its effectiveness.

OPS Is Changing How It Inspects Pipelines and Enforces Compliance With Regulations

OPS is moving toward inspecting entire pipelines rather than segments of pipelines and is reducing its reliance on fines to enforce compliance with its regulations. Since 1996, OPS has conducted 10 "systemwide inspections" to identify safety risks to companies' entire pipeline systems. These inspections require more time and resources per inspection than OPS' traditional approach, which is based on inspecting segments or "units" of pipelines. Partly because it was emphasizing systemwide inspections, OPS reduced the number of unit inspections by 47 percent from 1996 through 1999. Also as a result of systemwide inspections, OPS has decreased its reliance on state regulators to inspect interstate pipelines because the agency prefers to use a team of federal inspectors to conduct the systemwide inspections rather than coordinate the activities of federal inspectors and inspectors from multiple states. However, some state regulators are concerned that their diminishing role has resulted in fewer and less thorough inspections.

For enforcement, OPS has been decreasing its use of fines for pipeline companies' violations of safety regulations since before the 1996 act. From 1990 through 1998, OPS' use of fines decreased from 49 percent of total enforcement actions to 4 percent. According to OPS officials, this strategy allows them to focus their efforts and the companies' resources on correcting problems, but they have not evaluated whether their reduced reliance on fines is effective in achieving compliance with regulations.

OPS Is Changing Its Inspection Approach to Focus on Entire Pipeline Systems

Traditionally, OPS has inspected pipeline companies by conducting "unit inspections"—a checklist approach verifying that an individual operating unit of a company's entire pipeline system is in compliance with pipeline safety regulations. A unit inspection is generally conducted by one OPS inspector in about 3 days. Instead of relying primarily on a unit-by-unit approach to inspections, OPS is now inspecting pipelines through "systemwide inspections"—reviewing all of a company's related operating units at once. Because systemwide inspections can cover hundreds of miles of pipeline in various regions of the country, OPS uses a team of inspectors from all OPS regions that contain part of the operator's system to inspect all of the operating units. According to OPS officials, a systemwide inspection is the equivalent of multiple unit inspections. OPS conducted six systemwide inspections in 1998 and four in 1999; it plans to conduct eight in 2000.

According to OPS officials, systemwide inspections provide a better assessment of the potential safety risks to pipelines than do unit inspections because systemwide inspections can uncover problems that unit inspections would not identify. For example, according to OPS officials, one pipeline company did not coordinate its corrosion prevention activities with information it was obtaining from another part of the company on external damage. Such damage—e.g., a nick in a pipeline's protective coating—can lead to corrosion. During a systemwide inspection, OPS identified this lack of communication as a potential threat to the pipeline's safety.

Besides moving to systemwide inspections, OPS is spending more time on construction inspections to reduce the risk that defects will be built into pipelines during construction. Construction inspections also involve more OPS resources than do unit inspections because months may be needed to build a pipeline and inspectors must review plans and observe crucial points in the construction. Since 1995, both the number of pipeline construction inspections and the time OPS inspectors have spent on such inspections have increased. In 1999, OPS inspectors spent 546 days on 65 construction inspections, compared with 102 days on 30 inspections in 1995.

As a result of its change in inspection philosophy, OPS is conducting fewer unit inspections. The number of unit inspections conducted by OPS decreased by 47 percent from 1996 through 1999. (See fig. 5.) (The number of inspections increased sharply during 1995 and 1996 because additional inspectors were hired during that period; since that time, the staffing has remained level.) According to OPS officials, this decrease is due to the increased emphasis on systemwide and construction inspections, as well as an increase in the number of accident investigations and in the resources devoted to risk management projects. In addition, OPS officials told us that each unit inspection now takes more time than it did in the past because the agency has modified its inspection form to obtain more in-depth information on how the pipeline company is ensuring the pipeline's safety. For example, the new form requires the inspector to evaluate the overall quality of the operator's corrosion-control program.

Figure 5: OPS' Inspection Activity, by Type of Inspection, 1990-99

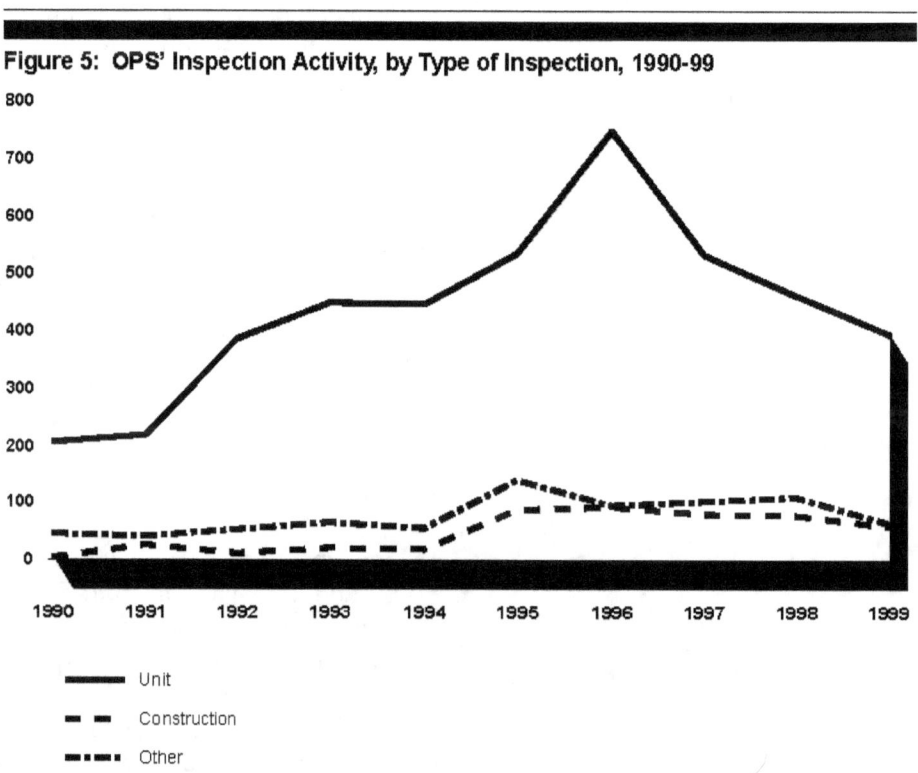

Note: "Other" includes failure investigations, complaint investigations, and systemwide inspections.

Source: GAO's analysis of OPS' data.

Also as a result of its change in inspection philosophy, OPS is relying less on states to inspect interstate pipelines. Although OPS is responsible for inspecting these pipelines, it certified some states to act as interstate agents in the early 1980s because it did not have enough inspection resources. From 1990 through 1994, about 12 interstate agents conducted between 20 and 26 percent of all interstate inspections. In 1995 and 1996, OPS hired additional inspectors and started taking back responsibility for these inspections. By 1999, only 8 percent of all interstate inspections were conducted by 10 interstate agents. In December 1999, OPS canceled its interstate agent agreements with Arizona and Nevada, leaving eight interstate agents—California, Connecticut, Iowa, Michigan, Minnesota, New York, Ohio, and West Virginia.[16]

According to OPS officials, the state agencies have performed well as interstate agents, but it is difficult to coordinate inspections by interstate agents—each responsible for the portion of a multistate pipeline system within its own borders—into a systemwide inspection. Rather than coordinating the activities of federal and state inspectors, OPS prefers to use a team of federal inspectors to conduct a systemwide inspection. In addition, OPS officials told us that devoting less time to their responsibilities as interstate agents would allow the states to focus their efforts on intrastate distribution pipelines, where most fatalities from pipeline accidents occur.

Some state officials do not agree with OPS' decision to eliminate interstate agents because they are concerned about its impact on safety. Even though interstate agents do not receive additional federal funds for inspecting interstate pipelines, officials from these states prefer to inspect these pipelines because it allows them to oversee the safety of all pipelines within their boundaries. Some current and prior interstate agents we contacted told us that they inspect operators more frequently than OPS— generally once every year compared with once every 1 to 4 years for OPS— and spend 2 to 4 times longer performing the inspections than does OPS. According to these officials, more frequent and more thorough inspections improve their ability to detect safety problems.

---

[16]In Mar. 2000, OPS proposed an agreement with the state of Washington involving the inspection of interstate pipelines, but, according to OPS officials, the state will not be an interstate agent.

In addition, some state officials are concerned that because OPS schedules all of its inspections in advance, some violations could go undiscovered. For example, a Connecticut pipeline safety official told us that the state's no-notice inspections on intrastate construction projects have discovered three times as many violations as advance-notice inspections. (According to an OPS official, OPS notifies the companies of the anticipated date of inspections so the companies can have the appropriate manuals and representatives available, but it does not tell the companies which portions of the pipelines will be examined.)

The Department of Transportation (DOT) has proposed legislation to reauthorize the pipeline safety program.[17] Among other things, this legislation would increase the ability of states to participate in the oversight of interstate pipeline transportation (including new construction inspections or accident investigations) and funding for these activities.

OPS Is Decreasing the Use of Fines for Violations

Since 1990, OPS has decreased its use of fines and increased its use of less severe corrective actions. According to OPS officials, this strategy allows them to work more constructively with companies to address problems. For example, instead of issuing a fine, OPS required a pipeline operator to hydrostatically test 350 miles of pipeline following an accident in 1993. The test revealed seven additional areas that were susceptible to future leaks. Fines are reserved for severe violations, such as those that have resulted in fatalities or substantial environmental damage, or for failures to address problems previously identified by OPS. OPS has not assessed the impact of this approach on safety.

The number of enforcement actions OPS has taken increased from 94 in 1990 to 218 in 1998—a 132-percent increase. However, OPS has also decreased the proportion of enforcement actions in which it proposed fines from about 49 percent in 1990 to about 4 percent in 1998. During this time, it increased the proportion of warning letters and letters of concern that are used to inform pipeline companies of probable violations of safety regulations or other pipeline safety risks but do not assess a fine. The proportion of enforcement actions in which these letters were sent increased from about 33 percent in 1990 to about 68 percent in 1998. (See fig. 6.)

---

[17]The Pipeline Safety and Community Protection Act of 2000 was introduced in the Senate on Apr. 12, 2000 (S. 2409) and the House on Apr. 13, 2000 (H.R. 4276).

Figure 6: Warning Letters/Letters of Concern and Fines as Percentages of Total Enforcement Actions, 1990-98

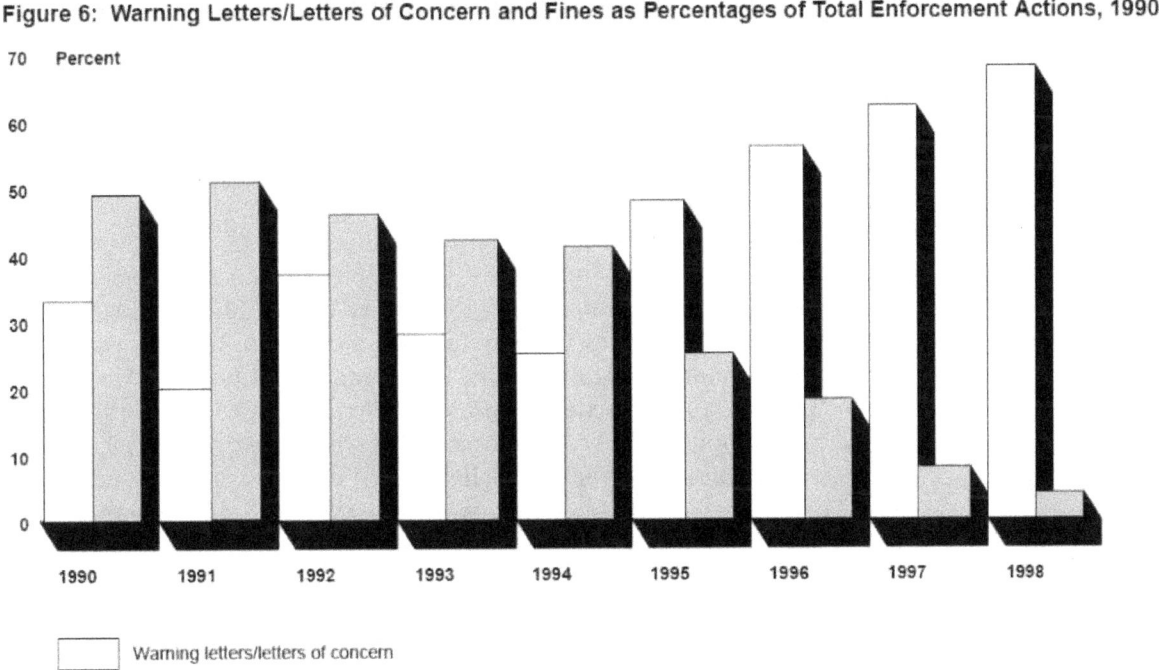

Warning letters/letters of concern

Fines

Note: The percentages for letters and fines do not add to 100 percent because OPS also uses other enforcement actions, such as compliance orders, to specify the actions a company must take to correct a violation. In addition, an enforcement action may include multiple actions, such as a fine and a compliance order.

Source: GAO's analysis of OPS' data.

According to OPS officials, the proportion of warning letters and letters of concern has increased because letters are now used to inform companies not only of compliance problems, but also of "best practices" that OPS believes would improve the safety of the companies' pipelines. These officials told us that the agency also relies heavily on other enforcement actions that do not involve fines, such as compliance orders requiring pipeline companies to take action to correct safety violations. However, OPS officials were not able to identify (1) how many letters addressed "best practices" rather than safety violations and (2) how many other enforcement actions did not involve fines.

OPS has not assessed the effectiveness of its reduced reliance on fines. However, OPS reported in 1997 that some other federal agencies—including the Federal Railroad Administration, the Federal Aviation

Administration, and the Occupational Safety and Health Administration—share OPS' philosophy concerning the use of fines. For example, the report noted that the Federal Railroad Administration generally gives a rail carrier the opportunity to correct a safety problem before formally citing the carrier for violations and suspends proposed penalties in return for the carrier's agreeing to take immediate corrective action. The report did not assess the extent to which federal agencies that agree with OPS' approach have reduced their reliance on fines.

While some state pipeline regulators share OPS' enforcement approach for the intrastate pipelines under their jurisdiction, others continue to use fines extensively as a deterrent to noncompliance. For example, a Michigan official told us that Michigan pipeline safety regulators typically do not impose fines. In 1998, the state imposed no fines, and in 1999, it imposed only three of about $1,000 each. According to the Michigan official, Michigan regulators have always believed that civil penalties are not a strong deterrent to noncompliance and the few fines that Michigan does impose are for more serious violations. In contrast, Ohio pipeline safety regulators believe fines are an effective enforcement tool. According to one Ohio pipeline safety official, over the past 7-8 years, Ohio has imposed an average of one fine per year for approximately $50,000. In Ohio, the amount of the civil penalty depends on the seriousness of the violation and the size of the operator, and the penalties have ranged from $300 to $125,000.

OPS' Responsiveness to the Safety Board's Recommendations and to Statutory Requirements Has Been Mixed

OPS has a mixed record in responding to the Safety Board's recommendations. Historically, it has had the lowest rate of any transportation agency for implementing these recommendations. Some of the recommendations that OPS has not fully implemented have dealt with issues that the Safety Board has repeatedly reported on, such as the use of safety valves to rapidly shut down pipelines after ruptures and periodic internal inspections of pipelines to identify defects. OPS has recently taken action to improve its responsiveness in several other areas that the Safety Board has addressed, including excavation damage, corrosion control, and data quality. While Safety Board officials are encouraged by these recent efforts, they remain somewhat skeptical of OPS because, in the Safety Board's opinion, OPS has not followed through on past promises to implement the Safety Board's recommendations.

Several federal statutes also address pipeline safety issues, including a number of those covered by the Safety Board's recommendations. Specifically, since 1988, the Congress has imposed 49 requirements designed to improve pipeline safety. OPS has not implemented 22 of these requirements, 12 of which date from 1992 and prior years.

OPS Has Not Fully Implemented the Safety Board's Recommendations, but May Be Improving Its Responsiveness

Since 1967, the Safety Board has made 243 recommendations to OPS in response to its investigations of significant pipeline accidents (such as those in which a fatality has occurred). According to the Safety Board, OPS implemented only 69 percent of these recommendations and has historically had the lowest response rate of any transportation agency. (See table 3.) However, because this measure includes data from over 30 years, it may not accurately reflect OPS' current efforts to implement the Safety Board's recommendations.[18]

---

[18]According to Safety Board officials, a measure to capture an agency's recent (e.g., within the last 5 years) efforts would not be meaningful because (1) many of the agency's actions in response to the recommendations would probably not be complete and (2) the agency might not follow through on promises to implement recommendations.

Table 3: Transportation Agencies' Implementation Rates for Safety Board Recommendations, 1967-99

Transportation agency	Total number of recommendations	Implementation rate (percent)
Maritime Administration	17	100
Secretary of the Department of Transportation	247	88
Federal Highway Administration	446	87
National Highway Traffic Safety Administration	278	87
Federal Aviation Administration	3,756	83
Federal Transit Administration	66	82
United States Coast Guard	1,162	74
Federal Railroad Administration	483	73
Research and Special Programs Administration	374	72
Office of Pipeline Safety (within the Research and Special Programs Administration)	243	69
Total/average rate	**6,829**	**81**

Note: The Research and Special Programs Administration also includes the Office of Hazardous Materials Safety, which has received 131 recommendations and whose implementation rate was 75 percent from 1967 through 1999.

Source: National Transportation Safety Board.

Many of the Safety Board's recommendations deal with recurring issues, such as the use of valves to rapidly shut down pipelines after a rupture, the need for periodic internal inspections of pipelines, and the need to ensure that pipeline operators are adequately trained to respond to emergencies. According to OPS officials, OPS rarely disagrees with the Safety Board on the issues covered in the recommendations. However, strong differences exist between the agencies on whether and how to implement the recommendations, as the following examples show:

- The Safety Board has issued 11 recommendations since 1971 on using valves to rapidly shut down the flow of product to a ruptured pipeline to mitigate damage. The Safety Board has recommended that OPS require the use of excess flow valves—valves that stop the flow of gas on smaller service lines, such as natural gas distribution lines, when the flow exceeds a specified amount—on all new single-family residential high-pressure service lines. In addition, the Safety Board continues to recommend that OPS require the use of automatic or remotely operated valves on high-pressure pipelines in urban or environmentally sensitive areas. OPS has been opposed to requiring the widespread use of valves because several cost/benefit studies showed that the costs to the industry of installing valves are generally greater than the expected benefits. However, according to Safety Board officials, OPS does not always consider the full range of benefits in its analyses. For example, OPS concluded that there was no significant benefit from installing remotely controlled valves on natural gas transmission pipelines because the gas ignites upon escape and a rapid shutdown would not prevent fire. However, in March 1994, a rupture on a natural gas transmission pipeline in Edison, New Jersey, resulted in a fire that injured 112 people and destroyed eight buildings. Damage from the accident exceeded $25 million. The Safety Board reported that operators of the pipeline were unable to shut down the gas flow to the rupture for 2-½ hours. Had the operator been able to promptly shut it down, the Safety Board stated, firefighters could have extinguished the fire sooner and the damage to the apartment buildings would have been significantly reduced. The proposed rule on enhanced protection of pipelines in high-consequence areas would require pipeline companies to consider the use of remotely operated valves in these areas.

- Three Safety Board recommendations in 1987 called for OPS to require operators to conduct periodic internal inspections of all pipelines to identify weaknesses or defects. Although OPS required, in 1994, that new pipelines be built to accommodate internal inspection tools, such as smart pigs, it has not yet established requirements for conducting internal inspections. OPS believes that its proposed rule on the enhanced protection of pipelines in high-consequence areas would address these recommendations. However, this rule would address pipelines only in areas with the highest risk of harming people or the environment. According to officials from the Safety Board, this rule would represent progress in improving the safety of pipelines in areas where the consequences of accidents are greatest, but it would not fully address the Safety Board's 1987 recommendation that OPS require periodic inspections of all natural gas and hazardous liquid pipelines for corrosion or other damage.

- Since 1987, the Safety Board has issued two recommendations urging OPS to ensure that operators are adequately trained to construct and operate pipelines and to respond to emergencies. In 1994, OPS issued a proposed rule that specified training requirements for operators. The pipeline industry and OPS' advisory committees responded that the training requirements in this proposed rule were too specific. Because of the negative response to the proposed rule, OPS began a negotiated rulemaking and issued a final rule in August 1999 that allows various methods of demonstrating that an operator is qualified. For example, the rule states that, until October 28, 2002, pipeline companies can rely solely on an operator's past performance to certify that the operator is qualified. However, the Safety Board was dissatisfied, noting that if an operator has not needed to respond to an emergency in the past, the operator's past performance might not be an accurate measure of emergency preparedness. According to OPS officials, the agency is more concerned with ensuring that pipeline operators are qualified than with the specific methods pipeline companies use to qualify their personnel.

In other areas, OPS has recently taken actions that are responsive to the Safety Board's recommendations on excavation damage, corrosion control, and data quality.

• Excavation damage—the leading cause of pipeline ruptures—has been the topic of 13 recommendations issued by the Safety Board since 1989. OPS has two primary initiatives to address this issue. As required by the Transportation Equity Act for the 21st Century, enacted in 1998, OPS issued a report in August 1999 that identified existing best practices to prevent damage to underground facilities. Furthermore, OPS unveiled a national public education campaign in June 1999, called "Dig Safely," that helps communities teach their citizens how to prevent damage to pipelines and underground utilities.
• To control corrosion, the Safety Board recommended in 1987 that OPS require operators of natural gas transmission and hazardous liquid pipelines to periodically conduct inspections capable of identifying corrosion-caused damage to pipelines. At that time, OPS required natural gas and hazardous liquid pipeline operators to inspect for corrosion on buried metallic pipe that had been exposed by excavation and, if corrosion was found on a hazardous liquid pipeline, the operator was required to dig up additional pipeline to determine the full extent of the corrosion. In October 1999, OPS issued a final rule that requires natural gas operators to follow the same procedures as hazardous liquid pipeline operators. OPS also plans to update corrosion-control practices for both gas and liquid pipeline regulations to incorporate the latest safety practices for protecting steel pipe from corrosion.

- OPS has several initiatives under way to improve the quality of the accident data reported by pipeline operators. OPS is conducting a pilot project with the American Petroleum Institute to encourage oil pipeline operators to voluntarily report more detailed information than OPS normally collects on accidents. For example, the pilot uses 20, rather than 5, categories of accident causes and lowers the threshold of accidents to be reported from 50 barrels of product spilled to 5 gallons spilled. Data from this pilot, which should begin to be available in the spring of 2000, may be better for analyzing trends in areas such as causes, property damage, and remediation costs. OPS has also drafted a new accident-reporting form for liquid pipeline accidents that incorporates the expanded categories of accident causes that are being used in the pilot, and it plans to modify the forms for natural gas transmission and natural gas distribution pipeline accidents. Finally, in a recent report, the Department of Transportation's Inspector General recommended that OPS collect more complete, detailed information on the causes of accidents, and OPS agreed to do so.[19]

OPS and Safety Board officials have been meeting biannually to discuss outstanding recommendations and work to resolve disagreements between the agencies. Safety Board officials have been pleased with many of OPS' actions and the improved communications between the agencies during the last year. However, many of the actions are incomplete, and some, such as OPS' proposed rule requiring the enhanced protection of high-consequence areas, will not fully address the recurring pipeline safety issues that have prompted the Safety Board's recommendations. Therefore, Safety Board officials are waiting to see the results of OPS' promised actions before assessing the extent to which OPS' responsiveness has improved.

OPS Has Not Fully Implemented Statutory Requirements

In addition to the Safety Board's recommendations, 49 congressional requirements have been imposed since 1988 to improve the safety of pipelines and enhance OPS' ability to oversee the pipeline industry.[20] (App. IV lists these pipeline safety statutory requirements and their status.) Twenty-two of these requirements have not been implemented, and 12 of

---

[19]*Pipeline Safety Program*, Office of Inspector General, U.S. Department of Transportation, RT-2000-069 (Mar. 13, 2000).

[20]The Senate and House Appropriations Committees have also directed OPS to carry out various activities in reports accompanying OPS' annual appropriations. Several of these directives reiterate the statutory requirements.

them date from 1988 to 1992. (See table 4.) Ten of these 12 requirements were to be completed by deadlines stated in the statutes and are now between about 5 and 11 years past these deadlines.

Table 4: Status of Implementation of Statutory Requirements, 1988-2000

Legislation	Total number of requirements	Number of requirements not complete
Pipeline Safety Reauthorization Act of 1988	11	3
Oil Pollution Act of 1990	1	0
Offshore Pipeline Navigational Hazards (1990)	6	1
Pipeline Safety Act of 1992	15	8
Accountable Pipeline Safety and Partnership Act of 1996	15	10
Transportation Equity Act for the 21st Century (1998)	1	0
Total	**49**	**22**

Source: GAO's analysis of pipeline safety legislation from 1988-2000.

The statutory requirements often addressed the same issues as the Safety Board's recommendations. For example, three requirements from 1988, 1992, and 1996 called for periodic inspections of pipelines, five requirements from 1988, 1992, and 1996 addressed the use of safety valves, and four requirements from 1988, 1992, 1996, and 1998 addressed excavation damage. These requirements also cover other issues. For example, in October 1992, the Congress required OPS to define by October 1994 areas unusually sensitive to environmental damage from a hazardous liquid pipeline rupture. According to OPS officials, the agency did not meet the statutory deadline because reaching a consensus with other federal agencies and environmental groups on a definition of these areas has been complicated by the broad range of definitions currently in use. OPS issued a proposed rule on a definition of areas unusually sensitive to environmental damage on December 30, 1999, and expects to complete the final rule by the end of 2000.

Both OPS and the Safety Board agree that there is a need to increase pipeline safety in the areas where the Safety Board has made recommendations—areas that are also frequently addressed by statutory requirements. The agencies' disagreement over several of the Safety Board's recommendations focus on how best to achieve that result. Although some disagreements remain, the Safety Board has been encouraged by OPS' recent actions to implement its recommendations and the statutory requirements. We believe that it is essential for OPS and the Safety Board to continue to work together to resolve their differences.

Conclusions

We are concerned that OPS is discontinuing the use of states to help conduct inspections of interstate pipelines primarily because of logistical difficulties in scheduling systemwide inspections when states are involved. States' familiarity with pipelines in their jurisdictions could aid in identifying the very risks that OPS is hoping to mitigate through its planned risk management approach to safety regulation. This familiarity could argue for states' participation in reviewing integrity management programs that pipeline companies would be expected to develop under a risk management approach. In addition, a combined federal and state approach to overseeing pipeline safety could better leverage federal resources.

OPS' approach of working constructively with pipeline companies and reducing its reliance on monetary penalties to enforce its regulations is consistent with the actions of several other federal regulators, such as the Federal Railroad Administration, as well as several state pipeline regulators. However, a reduction in enforcement actions that result in fines from nearly 50 percent to 4 percent represents a significant change in how OPS obtains compliance with pipeline safety regulations. If pipeline companies are achieving compliance through less punitive actions, then OPS' reduced reliance on fines may be reasonable. However, OPS has not assessed whether (1) less punitive actions are effective in achieving the desired results or (2) its actions to reduce reliance on fines go farther than other agencies' actions. An assessment of the degree to which OPS' change in approach to enforcement actions has maintained, improved, or lessened compliance with safety regulations could provide a basis to judge whether the agency is moving in the right direction.

Recommendations

We recommend that the Secretary of Transportation direct OPS to work with state pipeline safety officials to determine which federal pipeline safety activities would benefit from state participation and, for those states willing to participate, integrate state participation into these activities.

We further recommend that, if OPS issues a final rule requiring individual pipeline companies to develop integrity management programs, the Secretary should direct OPS to allow state inspectors to help review the programs developed by the companies that operate in their states to ensure that these companies have identified and adequately addressed safety risks to their systems.

Finally, we recommend that the Secretary of Transportation determine whether OPS' reduced use of fines has maintained, improved, or decreased compliance with pipeline safety regulations.

Agency Comments and Our Evaluation

We provided a draft of this report to DOT for its review and comment. We met with officials from DOT, including OPS' Director, Office of Policy, Regulations, and Training, to obtain their comments. The DOT officials generally agreed with the draft report's recommendations. The officials stated that ongoing regulatory and legislative activities demonstrate that efforts are under way to implement the draft report's recommendation that OPS work closely with the states and their pipeline inspectors to further improve the level of pipeline safety. For example, DOT's proposed legislation to reauthorize the pipeline safety program would include specific authority for states to participate in new construction inspections and accident investigations on interstate pipelines. The officials told us that DOT's initiatives are intended to enable state inspectors to better focus their oversight efforts and to improve OPS' interactions with the states. The officials also told us that DOT is moving to substantially increase the funding available for state inspection activities and, for the first time, provide funding for certain state inspection activities on interstate pipelines. We are pleased that DOT recognizes the importance of working cooperatively with the states in overseeing pipeline safety. However, we continue to believe that, in addition to new pipeline construction and accident investigations, DOT should specifically allow the states to participate in reviews of interstate pipeline companies' integrity management programs, as we recommended in the draft report.

According to the officials, while OPS increasingly favors the use of corrective action and other compliance orders, it maintains all traditional enforcement tools and applies them when necessary. Furthermore, the officials told us that DOT's proposal to reauthorize the pipeline safety program is intended to strengthen the enforcement tools available to OPS. The officials maintain that the new enforcement approach has obtained more immediate and thorough corrective and remedial actions than would have been obtained through an approach based solely on increased fines. We recognize that DOT's pipeline safety program reauthorization proposal is intended to strengthen the enforcement tools available to OPS. However, while DOT officials claim that OPS' new approach of using corrective action and other compliance orders in lieu of fines has achieved benefits that would not have been obtained otherwise, a formal assessment of this new approach, as we recommended in the draft report, is needed to determine whether it is providing an equal, greater, or lesser level of compliance with the regulations.

Finally, the officials emphasized that DOT will continue to require full regulatory compliance even as it moves to further refine its focus on risk. Under OPS' integrity management program for the enhanced protection of pipelines in high-consequence areas, DOT plans to supplement regulatory compliance with a comprehensive examination of individual pipeline systems to identify and act on potential risk factors. DOT told us that this approach will make use of expertise from all aspects of pipeline design, construction, and operation to integrate information in a supplemental evaluation of systemwide risk factors. Once the risks are identified, operators will be required to act on the assessment through repair, prevention, and mitigation. We modified our draft report to further clarify that OPS' proposed integrity management program for the enhanced protection of pipelines in high-consequence areas is intended to be a supplement to, rather than a replacement of, the existing pipeline safety regulations.

DOT officials also provided technical clarifications, which were incorporated as appropriate.

Scope and Methodology

To determine the extent of pipeline accidents from 1989 through 1998 (the most recent year for which data were available), we collected and analyzed OPS' data on pipeline accidents. We did not independently verify the reliability of the data. To ensure an objective comparison across all types of pipelines, we included in our analysis only those accidents that met the reporting criteria common to all types of pipelines—accidents that resulted in a fatality, an injury requiring hospitalization, or $50,000 or more in property damage. We defined these accidents as "major accidents." We also reviewed more extensive data on the causes of accidents compiled by the Association of Oil Pipe Lines, the American Petroleum Institute, and the American Gas Association.

To determine OPS' implementation of the risk management demonstration program, we reviewed the statutory requirements for the program and program documents maintained on OPS' web-based document management system, including program guidance and project applications. We also interviewed OPS officials and representatives from the pipeline companies participating in the program.

To describe OPS' inspection and enforcement efforts since the 1996 act, we reviewed data on OPS' inspections and enforcement actions from 1990 through 1998 and analyzed trends in these activities. We interviewed OPS officials and representatives from the pipeline industry and environmental groups. We conducted telephone interviews with state pipeline safety officials in 12 states that have acted as interstate agents within the last 5 years—Arizona, California, Connecticut, Iowa, Michigan, Minnesota, Nevada, Ohio, New York, Rhode Island, Utah, and West Virginia. We also visited three states—Texas, Virginia, and Washington—where major pipeline accidents were investigated by the Safety Board and officials have sought a greater role for states in pipeline safety.

To determine OPS' responsiveness to the National Transportation Safety Board's recommendations and statutory requirements, we reviewed the Safety Board's reports and recommendations since 1989, analyzed statistics on the recommendations since 1967, and discussed the results of our analysis with Safety Board and OPS officials. We did not assess the merits of the Safety Board's recommendations or the adequacy of OPS' response. We reviewed pipeline safety statutes, annual appropriations acts, related congressional committee reports, and reports by OPS to identify statutory requirements since 1988. We reviewed OPS' reports and analyses of the status of the requirements. We did not assess the adequacy of OPS' response to statutory requirements or independently verify the status of the requirements.

To determine the status of the ongoing investigation of the accident in Bellingham, Washington, we interviewed representatives and reviewed documents from the following agencies and groups: the National Transportation Safety Board, OPS' Western Region, the Washington Utilities and Transportation Commission, the Washington State Governor's Fuel Accident Prevention and Response Team, the city of Bellingham, SAFE Bellingham, and Olympic Pipe Line Company.

We conducted our work from August 1999 through April 2000 in accordance with generally accepted government auditing standards.

As arranged with your office, unless you publicly announce its contents earlier, we plan no further distribution of this report until 30 days after the date of this letter. At that time, we will send copies of the report to congressional committees and subcommittees responsible for transportation safety issues; the Honorable Rodney E. Slater, Secretary of Transportation; the Honorable Kelley S. Coyner, Administrator, Research and Special Programs Administration; the Honorable Jim Hall, Chairman, National Transportation Safety Board; the Honorable Jacob Lew, Director, Office of Management and Budget; and other interested parties. We will make copies available to others upon request.

If you or your staff have any questions about this report, please contact me at (202) 512-3650. Key contributors to this report are listed in appendix V.

Sincerely yours,

Phyllis F. Scheinberg
Associate Director, Transportation Issues

The Bellingham, Washington, Pipeline Accident

The Olympic Pipe Line Company operates a pipeline system consisting of about 400 miles of pipelines that transport petroleum products from refineries at Cherry Point, Ferndale, and Anacortes in northwestern Washington to Portland, Oregon, and intermediate delivery points. Products transported include gasoline, distillates (heating oil and diesel fuel), and jet fuel. The system is operated by remote control from an operations center located in Renton, Washington.

On June 10, 1999, one of Olympic's pipelines transporting gasoline ruptured in the Whatcom Falls Park area of Bellingham, Washington. About 250,000 gallons of gasoline from the pipeline entered the Hannah Creek and Whatcom Creek where the fuel was ignited, resulting in three fatalities and eight injuries. In addition, the banks of the creek were destroyed over a 1.5-mile section, and several buildings adjacent to the creek were severely damaged.

Pipeline Rupture on June 10, 1999

Although the investigation of the accident is ongoing, the National Transportation Safety Board (the Safety Board) and the Department of Transportation's Office of Pipeline Safety (OPS) have preliminarily reconstructed the events leading up to the pipeline rupture. Shortly before the rupture occurred, pipeline operators attempted to start a pump at the Woodinville pumping station to facilitate the smooth flow of gasoline through the pipeline. (See fig. 7.) The pump did not engage, and pressure started to build within the pipeline. A relief valve at the Bayview station was designed to divert the gasoline from the pipeline to a tank to relieve the increasing pressure, and a block valve, also located at the Bayview station, was designed to close and stop the flow of gasoline. The Safety Board believes that the block valve closed as it should have done. However, gasoline continued to be pumped into the pipeline at Cherry Point, causing the pressure in the pipeline segment between Cherry Point and Bayview to continue increasing. The pipeline subsequently ruptured about midway along the segment at the Bellingham water treatment plant, near Whatcom Creek.

Figure 7: Location of Olympic Pipe Line Rupture

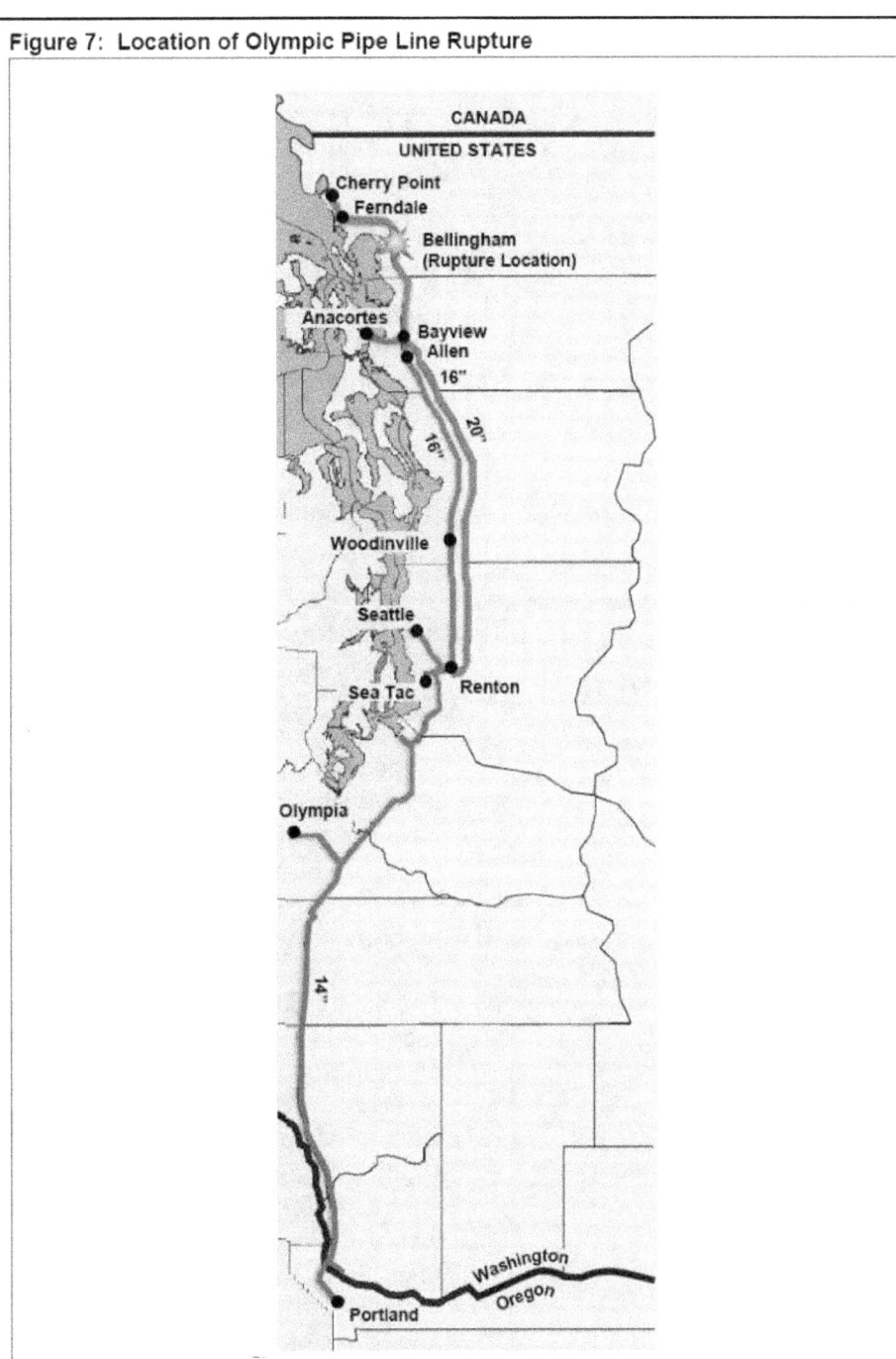

Source: National Transportation Safety Board.

According to the Chairman of the Safety Board, preliminary data show that when the rupture occurred, the pressure in the pipeline was well above normal operating levels. However, the pressure was substantially below the maximum pressure that a pipe of this design and size should have been able to withstand, and it was below the maximum allowable surge pressure permitted by regulatory standards.

According to Safety Board officials, the pipeline shut down after the rupture. However, Olympic Pipe Line controllers restarted the pipeline about 45 minutes later, and gasoline was pumped into the damaged segment for about 17 minutes. Between 250,000 and 300,000 gallons of gasoline (from the initial rupture and the subsequent restart of the pipeline) flowed from the damaged pipeline to the Hannah Creek and Whatcom Creek. Whatcom Creek—a salmon habitat—flows through Whatcom Falls Park in Bellingham.

The Safety Board's Investigation of the Accident

Investigators from the Safety Board are examining several factors that may have caused or contributed to the accident, including excavation damage, valve malfunctioning, operator training, and computer issues. However, several key activities in the Safety Board's investigation have been suspended because (1) Olympic Pipe Line Company employees with direct knowledge of the events have exercised their Fifth Amendment rights and have not responded to the Safety Board's questioning and (2) the Department of Justice halted destructive testing of the pipeline segment in order to preserve evidence. On April 5, 2000, the Safety Board was authorized to proceed with the testing of the pipeline segment.

The Safety Board's preliminary visual inspection of the ruptured pipeline segment indicated external damage to the pipeline at the point of rupture and additional damage to the area. In 1993 and 1994, a contractor working on behalf of the city of Bellingham installed new water lines across Olympic's pipeline at points approximately 20 feet and 10 feet south of the rupture. In 1991, an internal inspection of the pipeline did not identify any anomalies in the immediate vicinity of the rupture. However, two internal inspections conducted in 1996 and 1997 after the construction of the water lines identified several anomalies in the vicinity of the rupture. According to the Chairman of the Safety Board, Olympic Pipe Line indicated that the anomalies did not meet the applicable criteria for excavating the pipeline for a closer examination. The Safety Board is determining what criteria were used and plans to meticulously test the ruptured pipeline segment to determine whether external damage may have contributed to the rupture.

The Safety Board is also investigating the performance of the relief valve and the block valve at the Bayview station. Because Olympic modified the relief valve when it was installed, the Safety Board is examining whether the company followed the manufacturer's specifications for the modification. In addition, preliminary information indicates that the block valve had closed over 50 times in the 6 months prior to the accident, often because of pressure buildups similar to the one that occurred before the accident on June 10. The Safety Board is evaluating these events to determine the pressures involved, the functioning of the relief valve, and the possible impact of the pressure buildups on the overall integrity of the pipeline segment that ruptured.

The Chairman of the Safety Board also stated that the Safety Board wants to document and analyze the data available to controllers at the time of the accident. According to the Chairman, the controllers seem to have been unaware of the rupture for an extended period of time and the fact that they restarted the pipeline after the rupture suggests a significant performance failure. The Chairman noted that the Safety Board does not know whether this can be traced to insufficient training, inadequate qualifications, equipment malfunctions, poor design in the computer-based control system, or some other undetermined factor.

Finally, Olympic initially reported that the computer system that controls the pipeline experienced a "slowdown" during the accident that affected the ability of the controllers to observe the pipeline's functions and to change settings. The Safety Board's preliminary analysis of the computer tapes did not identify a slowdown. Olympic has reported that such a slowdown cannot be verified or reproduced.

OPS' Actions Following the Accident

On June 18, 1999, OPS issued a corrective action order to Olympic Pipe Line Company (owned and operated by Equilon Pipeline Company, LLC) which directed Olympic not to operate the damaged pipeline segment until the company, among other things, reviewed its computer system to determine the cause of the slowdown and take corrective action, tested mainline valves, and submitted a plan to OPS addressing factors that contributed to the rupture. The order also restricted the operating pressure on the remainder of the pipeline until OPS approves a return to normal operating pressure. The order was amended on August 10, 1999, and again on September 24, 1999, to address safety issues identified during the ongoing investigation. For example, the subsequent orders required Olympic to further reduce the pressure on certain pipeline segments, develop and implement a training program for controllers on the use of the computer system (including abnormal operations), and conduct hydrostatic tests of certain segments of the pipeline (draining the pipeline, filling it with water, and increasing the pressure within the pipeline to identify weak points). In addition to the corrective action order, OPS issued an advisory to all pipeline operators to check the adequacy of the computer resources devoted to monitoring and controlling their pipeline operations.

OPS inspectors have been monitoring Olympic's corrective actions. The inspectors are (1) working as a party to the Safety Board's investigation, (2) conducting an enforcement investigation, and (3) monitoring upgrades and repairs to the pipeline in accordance with the corrective action order. OPS also retained an independent expert to evaluate complex data from the internal inspections conducted in 1996 and 1997. In addition, OPS stationed a pipeline inspector in Washington State. This inspector will oversee the safety and environmental integrity of pipelines in the upper Northwest region and work on issues related to the Bellingham accident.

On January 18, 2000, Olympic asked OPS for permission to restart the pipeline. As of April 2000, OPS officials had sent a response to Olympic detailing areas where it needed to take additional actions before the pipeline could be returned to limited service. When OPS decides to allow Olympic to restart the pipeline, the pipeline will be brought back into service in incremental steps.

Actions Taken by the City of Bellingham and Its Citizens

Within a week after the accident, officials from the city of Bellingham realized that the agreement under which Olympic operated its pipeline within the city limits had expired. According to city officials, the need for Olympic to re-obtain the city's permission to operate its pipeline gave them some added leverage in negotiating several agreements with Olympic. The city extended the expired agreement until May 4, 2000, provided that Olympic complied with two other agreements between the city and Olympic—a safety action plan and a master agreement.

The safety action plan includes safety-related activities to be performed by Olympic before the section of the pipeline that ruptured can be restarted at reduced pressure, as well as activities to be performed at various stages after restarting the pipeline. These activities include (1) the testing of existing valves and installation of new valves; (2) hydrostatic testing of the pipeline; (3) computer testing and modifications; (4) the installation of an additional leak detection system; (5) an internal inspection of the pipe within 3 months of startup (and in any event no later than 6 months after startup); (6) field inspections and repairs based on the results of the internal inspection, and (7) a management audit to be performed by an independent party. OPS incorporated participation in the management audit into the September 24, 1999, amendment to its corrective action order.

On February 11, 2000, Olympic sent a letter to the city of Bellingham responding to the conditions for restarting the pipeline. The city continues to have concerns about Olympic's response.

The master agreement specifies that Olympic cannot restart the pipeline until it has satisfied the requirements in the city's safety action plan and OPS' corrective action order. In addition, the master agreement requires Olympic to study the feasibility of rerouting the pipeline around Bellingham. On February 1, 2000, Olympic submitted a report to the city in which it concluded that rerouting the pipeline was not feasible because it was unlikely that a new route would gain permitting approval from state and federal agencies. As of April 2000, the city had not responded to the report's conclusions.

One week after the accident, a group of citizens from Bellingham formed a group—SAFE Bellingham—to ensure that the creek would be restored, that Olympic would be held accountable, and that actions would be taken to mitigate future accidents. SAFE Bellingham has organized a coalition of communities that have experienced pipeline accidents to promote changes to federal pipeline safety regulations and has drafted a proposal for a local advisory committee to monitor pipeline safety within states.

Actions Taken by the State of Washington

The governor of Washington established a task team after the accident to evaluate pipeline safety within the state. The task team issued a report in December 1999 that recommends changes in law and practice at the federal, state, and local levels and changes in practice by fuel transmission pipeline operators in Washington. For example, the report recommends that the state pursue (1) federal regulation that would allow states to regulate the portions of interstate pipelines within their borders using standards more stringent than OPS', (2) federal legislation that would authorize states to receive higher levels of grant support from OPS, and (3) state executive branch and legislative changes that would strengthen pipeline safety.

As of April 2000, the state was working on an agreement with OPS regarding the inspection of interstate pipelines. On March 28, 2000, the governor signed a bill that establishes a statewide program to improve pipeline safety in Washington by having, among other things, the state's Utilities and Transportation Commission adopt new regulations and provide technical assistance to local governments. The bill also establishes a citizen advisory committee to help the public, local governments, and the industry work with the state on pipeline safety. Finally, the bill increases the penalties for failing to call a central number to identify the location of pipelines before digging.

Actions Taken by Olympic Pipe Line Company

In addition to responding to OPS' corrective action order and the city of Bellingham's safety action plan, Olympic issued a corridor safety action plan in October 1999 that applied many of the same actions being taken in the Bellingham area to the entire pipeline corridor from Ferndale to Portland. For example, Olympic's action plan includes requirements for valve testing and internal inspections along the entire pipeline.

Representatives from Olympic are on a committee with representatives from the city of Bellingham and other consultants to restore and improve Hannah and Whatcom creeks. Olympic has provided the initial funding for restoration and improvement efforts, which include erosion control, replanting, and building new salmon spawning pools. According to a member of the committee, Whatcom Creek's water quality has been restored and several species of salmon have been observed in the creek.

Barge and truck transport are being used to deliver petroleum products during the shutdown of the damaged pipeline segment. According to attorneys representing Olympic, maintaining delivery has been difficult at times, especially since Olympic is the sole supplier of jet fuel to the Seattle-Tacoma Airport.

Maps of Natural Gas Transmission and Hazardous Liquid Pipelines

Figure 8: Locations of Natural Gas Transmission Pipelines

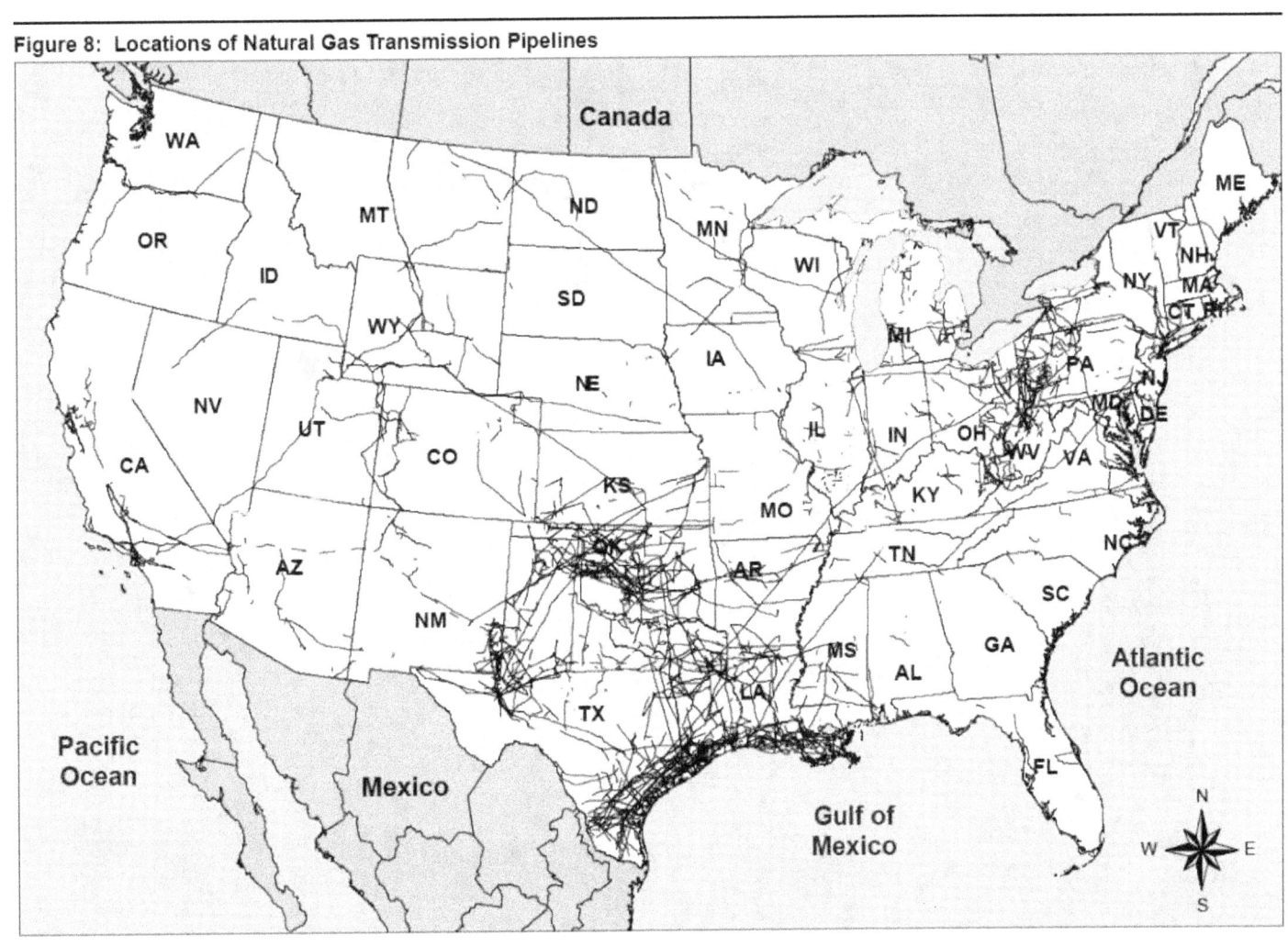

Source: OPS, based on data from MAPSearch Services

Figure 9: Locations of Hazardous Liquid Pipelines

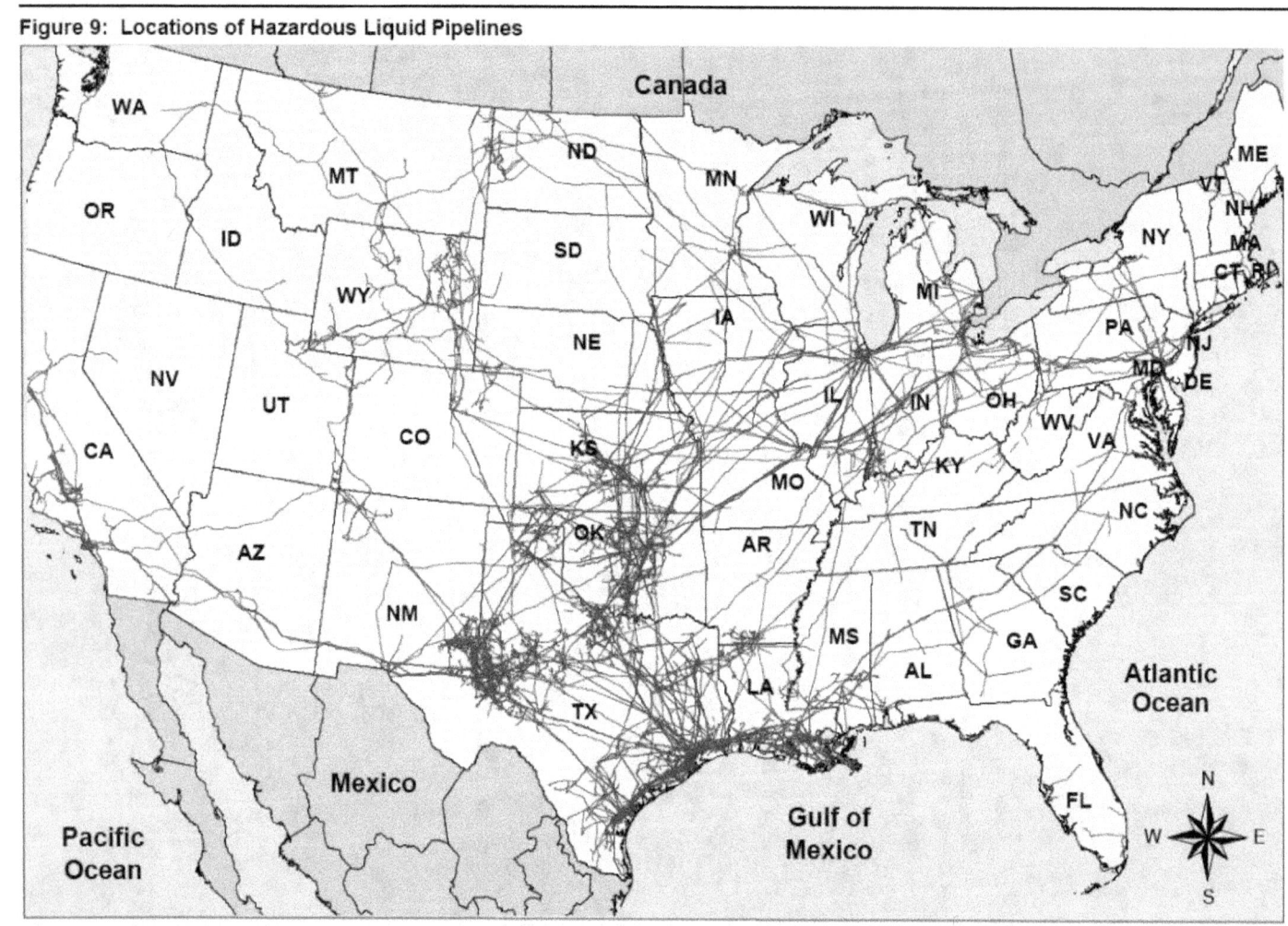

Source: OPS, based on data from MAPSearch Services.

Status of Risk Management Demonstration Projects

Since the inception of the risk management demonstration program, OPS has approved six pipeline companies' risk management projects for the program. These individual projects are designed to demonstrate the benefits of risk management under a variety of conditions, including differences in products, the ages of pipeline systems, environments, geography, and operating conditions (see table 5).

Table 5: Projects Approved for the Risk Management Demonstration Program

Operator	Regions affected	Project focus	Date approved
Equilon Pipeline	Southwest	Equilon is including two separate interstate pipeline systems in its project: a 205-mile segment of an ethylene pipeline and a 260-mile segment of a carbon dioxide pipeline. For these pipeline segments, Equilon is developing a comprehensive risk management program for assessing all hazards and risks associated with the operation of these pipelines. A major focus of the project is damage prevention during excavation and construction.	March 1998
Exxon Mobil	Central	Exxon Mobil is demonstrating its release prevention (tank integrity) program at its crude oil breakout facility in Patoka, Illinois. The project will examine how Exxon Mobil's release prevention measures will work in conjunction with OPS' proposed standards for aboveground storage tanks.	August 1998
Phillips Pipe Line Company	Southwest	Phillips is using risk management along a 60-mile segment of both an 18-inch and a 12-inch refined oil products pipeline. The project will explore ways of minimizing the risks associated with excavation work along the pipelines to reduce or eliminate damage from outside forces.	August 1998
Kinder Morgan, Inc.	Central, Southwest	The company is incorporating risk management into a 13,000-mile natural gas pipeline system. It hopes to form a comprehensive risk management program based on existing company programs such as pipeline integrity, regulatory compliance management, and emergency response.	December 1998
Chevron Pipe Line	Western	Chevron is including a 330-mile portion of its Salt Lake Products Pipeline System in the program. The system consists of two 8-inch product pipelines, one transporting gasoline and the other distillates such as diesel and jet fuel. Among other tasks, Chevron will conduct internal pipeline inspections and geologic hazard assessments of the pipelines for its project.	February 1999
Northwest Pipeline	Western	Northwest is developing a risk management program for its entire 3,900-mile natural gas system. The project will explore means of assessing and addressing risks presented by a pipeline in rugged terrain susceptible to land movement and investigate the risk-reduction benefits of certain new technologies.	January 2000

Source: GAO's analysis of information from OPS.

The direct federal costs of the risk management demonstration program are expected to be nearly $8 million from fiscal year 1996 through fiscal year 2000. According to OPS officials, OPS has not funded the participant companies' costs for the risk management demonstration projects but has incurred direct support costs for personnel, travel, and contractor support for evaluating and auditing the demonstration projects. In addition, OPS has provided grants to states totaling about $340,000 for travel costs associated with the projects. These direct support costs decreased from a total of about $1.8 million in fiscal year 1996 (the first year of the program) to about $1.4 million in fiscal year 1999, but they are expected to increase to about $1.6 million in fiscal year 2000, primarily because of increases in contractor support costs. (See table 6.)

Table 6: Federal Cost of the Risk Management Demonstration Program, by Fiscal Year

Description	Fiscal year					Total
	1996	1997	1998	1999	2000	
Federal salary and benefits[a]	$355,000	$363,000	$379,000	$393,000	$425,000	$1,915,000
Estimated travel costs	200,000	200,000	200,000	200,000	200,000	1,000,000
Contractor support costs	1,249,956	1,069,053	811,599	708,346	900,000[b]	4,738,954
State grants	0	40,000	100,000	100,000	100,000	340,000
Total	$1,804,956	$1,672,053	$1,490,599	$1,401,346	$1,625,000	$7,993,954

[a]Estimated salary and benefits for five full-time equivalent employees per year.

[b]According to OPS officials, this is an amount obligated for the 15-month period from Oct. 1, 1999, through Dec. 31, 2000.

Source: GAO's analysis of OPS' documents.

OPS' Action on Statutory Requirements, 1988-2000

This appendix consists of tables that summarize (1) the requirements for OPS established in six statutes and (2) the actions OPS has taken since 1988 in response to these requirements.

Table 7: Pipeline Safety Reauthorization Act of 1988 (P.L. 100-561, Oct. 31, 1988)

Section	Statutory requirement	Status
102 (gas) 202 (liquid)	Reporting standards: Within 1 year, establish standards for operators to provide information, including the following: Name, address, phone number; Map; Pipeline characteristics; Description of products transported; Operations manual; Emergency response plan.	Closed: 49 C.F.R. 192 and 195 require gas and hazardous liquid pipeline operators to (1) maintain records of the characteristics and maintenance history of their pipelines and (2) prepare an operations manual and an emergency manual. In addition, OPS, in conjunction with the National Pipeline Mapping System, has developed and published standards for collecting information on pipelines and their environment. OPS and the states are now receiving data from the pipeline companies. In addition, OPS is working with the hazardous liquid pipeline industry to develop a voluntary annual report that contains more information than is currently required, by regulation, from natural gas pipeline companies. This information will be provided to OPS by the end of 2000 through a voluntary data initiative of the American Petroleum Institute. The information anticipated from this ongoing initiative will likely make it unnecessary to require an annual report from hazardous liquid pipeline companies.
102 (gas) 202 (liquid)	Pipeline inventory: Establish standards to require operators, within 1 year, to complete and maintain an inventory of all types of pipe used, including the materials used and a history of any leaks.	Open: OPS formed a data team with the hazardous liquid pipeline industry to provide for the voluntary submission of data on pipeline facilities. During 1999, the hazardous liquid pipeline industry pilot-tested a system to assess the effects of the team's data collection recommendations; an analysis of the results will soon be completed. Pipe inventory standards for voluntary reporting are subject to further development. In 2000, OPS revised its annual report forms for gas and hazardous liquid transmission pipeline companies to provide better inventory information.
105(2) (gas) 209 (liquid)	Accident coordination: Within 1 year, establish procedures to more effectively coordinate the response of federal agencies and the states to pipeline accidents.	Closed: OPS coordinates accident response procedures with the National Transportation Safety Board, the Environmental Protection Agency, the Occupational Safety and Health Administration, the Coast Guard, the Federal Railroad Administration, and the Minerals Management Service through memorandums of understanding, letters of agreement, and informal undertakings. Parts 192 and 195 both require pipeline companies to provide information to local emergency response organizations to improve coordination during accidents. Liquid pipeline companies coordinate with federal response agencies and state and local agencies in planning for pipeline spills under the Oil Pollution Act. OPS participates in emergency response exercise programs.

Continued

Section	Statutory requirement	Status
108(a)(2) (gas) 207(a) (liquid)	Inspection frequency: Inspect and, as appropriate, require the testing of pipeline facilities at specified intervals, but no less frequently than once every 2 years; master meter operators can be inspected less frequently; the frequency and type of inspections shall be determined on a case-by-case basis, considering factors such as location, characteristics, and materials transported.	Closed: The Accountable Pipeline Safety and Partnership Act of 1996 (49 U.S.C. 60108(b)) eliminated the requirement for testing at 2-year intervals.
108(b) (gas) 207(b) (liquid)	Smart pig accommodation: Establish standards requiring that new and replacement pipe shall accommodate the passage of smart pigs.	Open for certain gas pipelines: A final rule for all pipelines was published (59 F. R. 17275, 4/12/94). Notice 2 (59 F.R. 49896, 9/30/94) extended the compliance date for existing gas transmission lines and modified the requirement for offshore and rural gas transmission lines. Notice 3 (60 F.R. 7133, 2/7/95) suspended enforcement of the final rule's requirements for modifications to sections of onshore gas transmission lines and for new and existing offshore gas transmission lines. A final rule in response to petitions for reconsideration is being prepared for publication in 5/00.
108(c)(gas)	Master meter study: Assess the need for an improved inspection program for master meter systems and issue a report within 18 months.	Open: A final report, An Analysis of Natural Gas Master Meter Systems (Definition and Program) from a Federal Perspective, was issued 6/15/79. An additional study on master meter systems was drafted following a survey of the states. The data on master meter systems included in the report are being updated. The report will be finalized and issued by the end of 2000.
211(a) (liquid)	Carbon dioxide: Regulate carbon dioxide transported by pipeline and amend regulations as appropriate to ensure the safe transportation of carbon dioxide by pipeline.	Closed: 49 C.F.R. part 195 was amended for carbon dioxide on 6/21/91.
303(a)	One-call systems: Within 18 months, issue regulations establishing minimum federal requirements for establishing and operating one-call notification systems for adoption by states.	Closed: 49 C.F.R. 198, Subpart C, 9/20/90 addresses one-call notification; also, 49 C.F.R. 192.614 and 49 C.F.R. 195.442, 11/19/97, mandate states' participation in one-call systems.
304	Smart pig feasibility study: Assess the feasibility of requiring the inspection of transmission facilities with smart pigs at periodic intervals and issue a report within 18 months.	Closed: OPS issued a report, Instrumented Internal Inspection Devices, in 11/92.
305	Emergency flow valve feasibility study: Study the safety, cost, feasibility, and effectiveness of requiring operators to install emergency flow-restricting devices and issue a report within 1 year.	Closed: A study sponsored by the Research and Special Programs Administration, Emergency Flow Restricting Devices Study, was issued in 3/91.
306	Feasibility of regulating excavation activity: Assess the feasibility of regulating persons whose excavation activities may result in damage to pipeline facilities and issue a report within 1 year.	Closed: A report, Examination of the Feasibility of Regulating Excavators, was issued in 10/90.

Continued from Previous Page

Source: For columns 1 and 2, GAO's analysis of pipeline safety statutes; for column 3, status reports from OPS.

Table 8: Oil Pollution Act of 1990 (P.L. 101-380, Aug. 18, 1990)

Section	Statutory requirement	Status
4202(a)(6), (b)(4)	Response plans for onshore oil pipelines: Issue regulations for oil spill response plans for onshore oil pipelines by 8/18/92.	Closed: An interim final rule on onshore facilities was published (58 F.R. 244, 1/5/93). Response plans have been submitted under this interim rule. The final rule, incorporating experience in operating spill response systems and reviewing plans, is to be issued in 5/00.

Source: For columns 1 and 2, GAO's analysis of pipeline safety statutes; for column 3, status reports from OPS.

Table 9: Offshore Pipeline Navigational Hazards (P.L. 101-599, Nov. 16, 1990)

Section	Statutory requirement	Status
1(a) (gas) 1(b) (liquid)	Reporting standards: Within 6 months of 11/16/90, establish standards defining "exposed pipeline facility" and "hazard to navigation."	Closed: 49 C.F.R. 192.3 and 195.2 define these terms.
1(a) (gas) 1(b) (liquid)	Hazardous conditions: Establish, by regulation, a program requiring operators of offshore and navigable water pipelines to report potential or existing navigational hazards involving pipeline facilities to the Secretary through the Coast Guard (as enacted, limited to the Gulf of Mexico and its inlets).	Closed: 49 C.F.R. 191.27, 192.612, 195.57, and 195.413 specify reporting procedures for pipelines in the Gulf of Mexico and its inlets. In addition, OPS issued alert notices to the offshore fishing industry (ALN-90-01) warning of hazards to fishing vessels from exposed pipelines and to Gulf of Mexico operators (ALN-98-03) warning of the possibility of exposed pipelines after Hurricane Georges.
1(a) (gas) 1(b) (liquid)	Permanent inspections: Establish an inspection program for offshore and navigable water pipelines no later than 30 months after 11/16/90 (as enacted, limited to the Gulf of Mexico and its inlets).	Open: OPS signed a memorandum of understanding with the Minerals Management Service to define inspection responsibilities for offshore pipelines. A proposed rule for periodic underwater pipeline inspections is now being prepared for publication by mid-2000.
1(a) (gas) 1(b) (liquid)	Burial: Require, by regulation, that exposed or hazardous pipelines be buried within 6 months after the date that the condition of the pipeline is reported to the Secretary (unless the Secretary extends the time period for compliance).	Closed: 49 C.F.R. 192.612 and 195.413 impose requirements for pipelines in the Gulf of Mexico and its inlets.

Continued

Section	Statutory requirement	Status
2	Navigational hazards: Establish a program to encourage fishermen and other vessel operators to report potential or existing navigational hazards involving pipelines to the Secretary through Coast Guard field offices.	Closed: 49 C.F.R. 191.23, 191.25, 192.27, 192.612, 192.615, 195.52-.58 establish procedures for reporting accidents and safety-related conditions for both gas and hazardous liquid pipelines. OPS issued a report, *Safety-related Condition Reporting*, in 7/88. In addition, OPS issued alert notices to the offshore fishing industry (ALN-90-01) warning of hazards to fishing vessels from exposed pipelines and to Gulf of Mexico operators (ALN-98-03) warning of the possibility of exposed pipelines after Hurricane Georges. Fishermen in the Gulf of Mexico now voluntarily provide reports on fishing net snags (which may or may not be on a pipeline), known as "hang" reports. These reports may result in compensation if the Minerals Management Service determines that a hang is on a pipeline facility. Louisiana also maintains its own Fisherman Gear Fund to compensate fishermen for lost nets and equipment in case of hangs on pipelines or production facilities.
3	Study: Study several issues related to underwater pipelines and report to the Congress on the results of actions no later than 6 months after 11/16/90.	Closed: OPS (1) informed operators and fishermen of the problems posed by exposed underwater pipelines and required the reporting of safety-related conditions, (2) completed its collection of computer-assisted maps of all offshore oil and gas lease blocks, (3) contracted with Texas A&M University for a study, issued in 1/98. The study recommended that OPS (1) establish regulations requiring the inspection of pipelines to determine their depth of burial and any need for reburial, (2) use risk analysis to determine the periodicity of future surveys, and (3) require operators to maintain pipelines 3 feet below the natural bottom and develop a mandatory one-call system for marine pipelines. OPS is drafting a proposed rule that will incorporate these recommendations.

Continued from Previous Page

Source: For columns 1 and 2, GAO's analysis of pipeline safety statutes; for column 3, status reports from OPS.

Table 10: Pipeline Safety Act of 1992 (P.L. 102-508, Oct. 24, 1992)

Section	Statutory requirement	Status
102(a)(2) (gas) 202(a)(2) (liquid)	<u>High-density population areas (for gas and liquid) and environmentally sensitive areas (for liquid)</u>: Within 2 years, issue regulations establishing criteria for the identification of all pipeline facilities that are located in high-density and environmentally sensitive areas.	<u>Open</u>: On 4/24/00, OPS issued a proposed rule requiring additional testing, inspection, and remediation of hazardous liquid pipelines in high-consequence areas. The agency issued, on 12/30/99, a proposed rule defining U.S. areas unusually sensitive to environmental damage (64 F.R. 73464). (Comments are due on 6/27/00). An additional proposed rule for the inspection and testing of gas transmission pipelines in high-consequence areas will be issued in 2000.
103(5) (gas) 203(5) (liquid)	<u>Update inspections/smart pigs</u>: Within 3 years, issue regulations requiring the periodic inspection of pipelines in high-density and environmentally sensitive areas, specifying the circumstances, if any, under which inspections should be conducted using smart pigs; when smart pigs are not required, require an inspection method that is at least as effective in providing for the safety of the pipeline.	<u>Open</u>: A proposed rule to require periodic inspections of hazardous liquid pipelines in high-consequence areas was issued on 4/24/00.
104 (gas)	<u>Excess flow valves</u>: (1) Within 18 months, issue regulations prescribing the circumstances, if any, under which operators must install excess flow valves; (2) within 2 years, issue regulations requiring operators to notify, in writing, customers whose lines do not require but can accommodate excess flow valves that such valves shall be installed at the request of the customer if the customer will pay all costs; (3) if there are no circumstances under which operators must install excess flow valves, issue a report within 30 days of such a determination on the reason for the determination; and (4) within 18 months, develop standards for the performance of excess flow valves used to protect lines in natural gas distribution systems.	<u>Closed</u>: A study found that excess flow valves were not cost-effective, and OPS did not require operators to install excess flow valves. However, 49 C.F.R. 192.383, 2/3/98, addresses requirements for notifying customers of the availability of excess flow valves, and 49 C.F.R. 192.381, 6/20/96, addresses performance standards for the valves.
212 (liquid)	<u>Emergency flow restriction devices</u>: (1) Within 2 years, survey and assess the effectiveness of emergency flow restriction devices (including remotely controlled valves and check valves) and other procedures, systems, and equipment used to detect and locate pipeline ruptures and minimize product releases from pipeline facilities; (2) within 2 years after the survey and assessment, issue regulations prescribing the circumstances under which operators must use emergency flow restriction devices and other procedures, systems, and equipment.	<u>Open</u>: OPS issued a proposed rule to solicit data (59 F.R. 2802, 1/19/94). A study sponsored by the Research and Special Programs Administration on emergency flow restriction devices was issued on 9/29/95. A public workshop was held in 10/95. The American Petroleum Institute's leak detection practices were adopted in 49 C.F.R. part 195 on 7/6/98. A proposed rule to require additional testing, inspection, and remediation of hazardous liquid pipelines in high-consequence areas was to be issued by 3/31/00. The American Petroleum Institute is to develop an industry standard on U.S. areas unusually sensitive to damage from a pipeline spill, which may help define pipeline segments, including those in high-consequence areas, that are candidates for emergency flow restriction devices and other inspection, testing, and integrity assurance approaches.

Continued

Section	Statutory requirement	Status
106(1) (gas) 205(1) (liquid)	Operator testing: Require testing and certification that addresses the ability to recognize and appropriately react to abnormal operating conditions that may indicate a dangerous situation or a condition exceeding design limits.	Closed: A final rule, to require all pipeline operations and maintenance workers to be qualified to perform their tasks and to be able to recognize and react to abnormal operating conditions, was published on 8/27/99 (64 F.R. 46853). Operators must have qualification plans prepared by 4/27/01 and all workers must be qualified by 10/28/02.
107 (gas)	Replacement of cast iron pipelines: Publish a notice as to the availability of industry guidelines for the replacement of cast iron pipe and, within 2 years after the guidelines are available, survey operators with cast iron piping systems to determine the extent to which each operator has adopted and followed a plan for the safe management and replacement of cast iron, the elements of the plan, and the progress that has been made.	Closed: OPS issued an alert notice (ALN-91-02) reminding all operators of natural gas distribution systems to have a program to identify and replace cast iron piping systems that may threaten public safety. The agency also informed operators of guidelines and computer programs that were available to help operators determine the serviceability of cast iron pipe and schedule its replacement. Cast iron is used exclusively by gas distribution operators that are regulated under state pipeline safety programs. Therefore, OPS' annual auditing of the state pipeline safety programs ensures that the states are monitoring distribution pipeline operators' plans for inspecting, managing, and replacing cast iron pipe. A survey of cast iron pipe in use by operators was completed in 1992 and is now being revised.
109(b) (gas) 208(b) (liquid)	Gathering lines: Within 2 years, issue a regulation defining a "gathering line" and within 3 years, issue a regulation defining a "regulated gathering line."	Open: A proposed rule defining a gas gathering line is expected by mid-2000.
115 (gas)	Customer-owned service lines: (1) Within 1 year, issue regulations requiring operators that do not maintain customer-owned service lines up to the walls of customers' buildings to advise their customers of the requirements for maintaining those lines; (2) within 18 months, review the Department of Transportation's and states' rules, policies, procedures, and other measures concerning the safety of customer-owned service lines and their effectiveness and survey the owners of customer-owned service lines regarding the operation and maintenance of such lines; (3) within 2 years, issue a report on the results of the review and survey; and (4) within 1 year after transmitting the report, take action to promote the adoption of measures to improve the safety of such service lines.	Closed: 49 C.F.R. 192.16, 8/14/95, imposes requirements for notifying customers. The requirement to take action to promote the adoption of measures to improve the safety of customer-owned service lines was eliminated in the Accountable Pipeline Safety and Partnership Act of 1996 (49 U.S.C. 60113).
108(5) (gas) 207(5) (liquid)	Periodic underwater inspections: Require operators to conduct periodic inspections of offshore pipelines and those in navigable waterways; within 2 years, define what constitutes an exposed underwater pipeline and what constitutes a hazard to navigation or public safety.	Open: A proposed rule (based on the Texas A&M University report's recommendation for a risk-based approach) is to be issued by 7/00.
113(a) (gas) 213(a) (liquid)	Opportunity for state comment: Provide to appropriate state officials in any state in which a pipeline facility is located notice and an opportunity to comment on any agreement proposed to be entered into by the Secretary to resolve a proceeding initiated under this section with respect to such a pipeline facility.	Closed: OPS provides an opportunity for state officials to comment before any agreement with a pipeline company is finalized. This is required by OPS' enforcement manual.

Continued from Previous Page

Section	Statutory requirement	Status
117 (gas) 216 (liquid)	Underwater abandoned pipeline facilities: Identify what constitutes a hazard to navigation with respect to underwater abandoned pipeline facilities and, within 18 months, specify the manner in which operators shall report underwater abandoned pipeline facilities.	Open: A proposed rule was published on 8/30/99 (64 F.R. 47157). The final rule was to be published by 4/00.
206 (liquid)	Low internal stress hazardous liquid pipeline facilities: In exercising discretion, the Secretary shall not provide an exception to regulation for any pipeline facility solely on the basis of the fact that such a pipeline facility operates at low internal stress.	Closed: A final rule, issued on 7/12/94, eliminated an exemption from regulation based solely on low internal pipe stress (59 F.R. 35465). Subsequently, questions were raised about the applicability of the rule to very short segments of pipeline carrying petroleum between plant sites. A proposed rule (63 F.R. 9993, 2/27/98) and a final rule (63 F.R. 46692, 9/2/98) addressed very short plant lines.
304	One-call enforcement: Establish procedures to notify the Occupational Safety and Health Administration of any pipeline accident in which an excavator, by causing damage to a pipeline, may have violated the Administration's regulations.	Closed: OPS monitors telephone reports from pipeline operators on a daily basis. Any report of an accident involving damage by an excavator or outside force is reported to the appropriate Occupational Safety and Health Administration regional office.
306	Underground utility location technologies: Carry out a research and development program on these technologies.	Open: Funding for research on pipeline-locating and -monitoring technologies is included in OPS' fiscal year 2001 budget request as part of the agency's proposed research program. The funding is not for a specifically authorized item but is included as part of OPS' research plan for preventing excavation damage.
307	Underwater abandoned pipeline facilities: Undertake a study of such facilities and, within 3 years, submit a report to the Congress on the results of the study.	Open: The Research and Special Programs Administration analyzed the extent and nature of the hazards posed by underwater abandoned pipelines and surveyed federal policies and state activities involving abandoned pipelines in navigable waters. The collected information proved to be insufficient to fully address the issue. Therefore, the Administration issued a proposed rule (64 F.R. 47157, 8/30/99) to require the reporting of abandoned pipelines. The Administration intends to continue analyzing the hazards posed by abandoned pipelines after it issues the final rule requiring the reporting of abandoned pipelines, expected by 6/00.

Continued from Previous Page

Source: For columns 1 and 2, GAO's analysis of pipeline safety statutes; for column 3, status reports from OPS.

Table 11: Accountable Pipeline Safety and Partnership Act of 1996 (P.L. 104-304, Oct. 12, 1996)

Section	Statutory requirement	Status
49 U.S.C. 60101(b)(2) 3(b)	Gathering lines: Amend the requirement to define "regulated gathering line" by changing "shall" to "shall, if appropriate."	Open: OPS is consulting with the gas pipeline industry and gathering line operators on alternative approaches to clearly identify gathering lines. A proposed rule is expected by 7/00.
60102(a) 4(a)(2),(3)	Operator qualification: Change a requirement to ensure that individuals performing operations and maintenance on pipelines are properly qualified by replacing the words "test and certify" with "qualified" and define qualifications to include the ability to recognize and react appropriately to abnormal operating conditions.	Closed: A final rule was published on 8/27/99. Operators must have plans prepared by 4/27/01, and all workers must be qualified by 10/28/02.
60102(b) 4(b)	Factors for consideration, including risk assessment and cost/benefit analysis: Clarify requirements to consider risk assessment, the environment, cost-benefit analysis, and the recommendations of advisory committees when prescribing standards, as well as a general requirement that standards be practicable and designed to meet needs for safety and environmental protection.	Closed: OPS' cost-benefit analyses were already in compliance with most of these requirements. In 2/99, OPS published guidance for cost-benefit analyses, *Final Report: A Collaborative Framework for Office of Pipeline Safety Cost-Benefit Analyses*, developed with input from the pipeline industry and opportunity for public comment. The advisory committees are acting as "peer reviewers" for all risk assessments and cost-benefit analyses prepared by OPS to support rulemaking actions. OPS provided the advisory committees with training in risk assessment and pipeline technologies to enable the committees to fulfill their roles.
60102(b)(7) 4(b)	Risk assessment: Not later than 3/31/00, transmit to the Congress a report that (1) describes the implementation of the act's risk assessment requirements and (2) includes any recommendations that would make the risk assessment process a more effective means of assessing the benefits and costs associated with alternative regulatory and nonregulatory options in prescribing standards.	Open: OPS provided an interim report, *Beyond Compliance: Creating a Responsible Regulatory Environment that Promotes Excellence, Innovation, and Efficiency: A Progress Report on the Pipeline Risk Management Demonstration Program*, to the Congress and the public in 5/99. The agency is now clearing a final report for issuance.
60102(f)(1) 4(e)	Standards on accommodating smart pigs: Require new and replacement natural gas transmission and hazardous liquid pipelines to accommodate "smart pigs"; allow the extension of such standards to existing pipelines.	Open for certain pipelines: A final rule was published (59 F.R. 17275, 4/12/94). Notice 2 (59 F.R. 49896, 9/30/94) extended the compliance date for existing gas transmission lines and modified the requirement for offshore and rural gas transmission lines. Notice 3 (60 F.R. 7133, 2/7/95) suspended OPS' enforcement of the final rule's requirements for modifications of sections of onshore gas transmission lines and for new and existing offshore gas transmission lines. A final rule addressing a petition for reconsideration is being prepared for publication in 5/00.
60102(f)(2) 4(e)	Periodic inspections: Modify the requirement for the Secretary to prescribe periodic inspections of each pipeline identified in high-density and environmentally sensitive areas by inserting "if necessary, additional" after "shall prescribe."	Open: A proposed rule to require periodic inspections of hazardous liquid pipelines in high-consequence areas was issued on 4/24/00.

Continued

Section	Statutory requirement	Status
60102(l) 4(f)	Updating standards: To the extent appropriate and practicable, update the standards incorporated by the industry that have been adopted as part of the federal pipeline safety regulatory program.	Open: OPS planned to issue a proposed rule in 12/99.
60102(c)(4) 4(g)	Promoting public awareness: (1) By 6/1/98, survey and assess certain public education and public safety programs and determine their effectiveness; (2) not later than 1 year after the survey and assessment are completed, institute a rulemaking to determine the most effective components of a public safety and education program and promulgate, if appropriate, standards implementing these components on a nationwide basis; (3) if the promulgation of such standards is not appropriate, report to the Congress the reasons for that finding.	Closed: A survey of damage prevention programs was completed in 1998, and a damage prevention pilot project has been completed in three states. OPS is working with the pipeline industry to evaluate existing public education programs. In 6/99, OPS "rolled out" a national promotional campaign.
60102(j)(3) 4(b)	Remotely controlled valves: (1) By 6/1/98, survey and assess the effectiveness of remotely controlled valves to shut off the flow of natural gas in the event of a rupture and (2) determine whether the use of remotely controlled valves is technically and economically feasible and would reduce the risks associated with a rupture; (3) within 1 year of completing the survey and assessment, if the use of valves is feasible and would reduce risks, prescribe standards for the use of these valves, including requirements for their use in densely populated areas.	Open: OPS published a report in 9/99 concluding that remotely controlled valves are technically, but not economically, feasible. At a public meeting on 11/4/99, OPS proposed that criteria, such as a definitive time to shut off a ruptured section in a high-consequence area, be considered. This issue will be considered further after high-consequence areas for gas transmission pipelines are defined.
60109(b) 7(b)	Unusually sensitive areas: Change language from "shall include" to "shall consider" under areas to be included as unusually sensitive; add drinking water and wildlife resources as considerations; and delete earthquakes and other ground movement as considerations.	Open: A proposed rule on the definition of unusually sensitive areas was issued (64 F.R. 73464, 12/30/99). (Comments are due on 6/27/00.)
60110(b)(4) 8(2)	Excess flow valves: Consider the costs of operation and maintenance in promulgating regulations requiring excess flow valves.	Closed: OPS adopted performance standards for excess flow valves and issued a rule requiring that customers be notified of the availability of such valves.
60126 5(a)	Risk management: Establish risk management demonstration projects and report on the results of such projects by 3/31/00.	Open: These projects are ongoing; OPS was preparing a final report for publication by 4/30/00.
60124 15(2)	Biennial reports: Not later than 8/15/97 and every 2 years thereafter, submit to the Congress a report on how this chapter was carried out during the 2 immediately preceding calendar years for gas and hazardous liquids.	Open: The first report was issued in 8/97; the next report was due in 8/99.

Continued from Previous Page

Section	Statutory requirement	Status
60127(a) 16(a)	Population encroachment: (1) Make available to each state the land-use recommendations in the Transportation Research Board's special report entitled *Pipelines and Public Safety* (No. 219); (2) evaluate the recommendations, determine the extent to which they are being implemented, consider ways to improve their implementation, and consider other initiatives to make local planning and zoning entities more aware of issues involving the encroachment of population along pipeline rights-of-way.	Open: OPS sent the Transportation Research Board's report to all states. An evaluation was to be prepared and published in early 2000.
60301(nt) 17	User fee assessment: Within 1 year, transmit to the Congress a report analyzing the present assessment of pipeline safety user fees solely on the basis of mileage to determine whether this or another measure would be more appropriate.	Closed: A draft report was approved by the pipeline safety advisory committees in 5/97. A final report was prepared and submitted to Congress in 3/98.

Continued from Previous Page

Source: For columns 1 and 2, GAO's analysis of pipeline safety statutes; for column 3, status reports from OPS.

Table 12: Transportation Equity Act for the 21st Century (P.L. 105-178, June 9, 1998)

Section	Statutory requirement	Status
7302(a) 49 U.S.C. 6105	One-call notification systems: If information is readily available, undertake a study of damage prevention practices associated with existing one-call notification systems and, within 1 year of enactment of this chapter, publish a report on the practices that are most and least successful.	Closed: A study of best practices to prevent damage to underground facilities, *Common Ground: Study of One-Call Systems and Damage Prevention Best Practices*, was published in 8/99. More than 160 government employees and underground facility operators contributed to the report. Follow-up action to establish a foundation for implementing the recommendations and best practices is now being established.

Source: For columns 1 and 2, GAO's analysis of pipeline safety statutes; for column 3, status reports from OPS.

GAO Contacts and Staff Acknowledgements

GAO Contacts

Phyllis F. Scheinberg (202) 512-3650
James Ratzenberger (202) 512-3650

Acknowledgements

In addition to those named above, Sumikatsu Arima, Ryan T. Coles, Helen Desaulniers, Deena Richart, and Sara Vermillion made key contributions to this report.

Ordering Information

The first copy of each GAO report is free. Additional copies of reports are $2 each. A check or money order should be made out to the Superintendent of Documents. VISA and MasterCard credit cards are accepted, also.

Orders for 100 or more copies to be mailed to a single address are discounted 25 percent.

Orders by mail:
U.S. General Accounting Office
P.O. Box 37050
Washington, DC 20013

Orders by visiting:
Room 1100
700 4th St. NW (corner of 4th and G Sts. NW)
U.S. General Accounting Office
Washington, DC

Orders by phone:
(202) 512-6000
fax: (202) 512-6061
TDD (202) 512-2537

Each day, GAO issues a list of newly available reports and testimony. To receive facsimile copies of the daily list or any list from the past 30 days, please call (202) 512-6000 using a touchtone phone. A recorded menu will provide information on how to obtain these lists.

Orders by Internet:
For information on how to access GAO reports on the Internet, send an e-mail message with "info" in the body to:

info@www.gao.gov

or visit GAO's World Wide Web home page at:

http://www.gao.gov

To Report Fraud, Waste, or Abuse in Federal Programs

Contact one:

- Web site: http://www.gao.gov/fraudnet/fraudnet.htm
- e-mail: fraudnet@gao.gov
- 1-800-424-5454 (automated answering system)

United States
General Accounting Office
Washington, D.C. 20548-0001

Official Business
Penalty for Private Use $300

Address Correction Requested